FOLLOWING THE MONEY

Following the Money
Comparing Parliamentary Public Accounts Committees

Dr Rick Stapenhurst,
Dr Riccardo Pelizzo
and Professor Kerry Jacobs

Commonwealth Parliamentary Association
with

First published 2014 by Pluto Press
345 Archway Road, London N6 5AA

www.plutobooks.com

Distributed in the United States of America exclusively by
Palgrave Macmillan, a division of St. Martin's Press LLC,
175 Fifth Avenue, New York, NY 10010

Commonwealth Parliamentary Association
Suite 700, Westminster House
7 Millbank, London SW1P 3JA

Copyright © 2014 Commonwealth Parliamentary Association

The right of Rick Stapenhurst, Riccardo Pelizzo and Kerry Jacobs
to be identified as the authors of this work has been asserted by them
in accordance with the Copyright, Designs and Patents Act 1988

British Library Cataloguing in Publication Data
A catalogue record for this book is available from the British Library

Library of Congress Cataloging in Publication Data applied for

ISBN 978-0-7453-3436-3 hardback

This book is printed on paper suitable for recycling and made from
fully managed and sustained forest sources. Logging, pulping
and manufacturing processes are expected to conform to the
environmental standards of the country of origin.

Produced for the Commonwealth Parliamentary Association
and Pluto Press by Chase Publishing Services Ltd
Simultaneously printed digitally by CPI Antony Rowe, Chippenham, UK
and Edwards Bros in the United States of America

Contents

About the Authors	vi
Secretary-General's Foreword	viii
Chairman's Foreword	xi
Preface	xiii

1	Introduction	1
2	Looking Backwards – McGee and the First CPA-WBI Study Group on Public Accounts Committees	18
3	The Structure of Public Accounts Committees	34
4	The Activities of PACs	48
5	Capacity of PACs	65
6	Developing Countries and Smaller Parliaments	83
7	The Changing World of PACs	92
8	The Political Will for Parliamentary Oversight	110
9	A Best Practice Guide for PACs	122

Afterword	143
Appendix: A Conceptual Framework	148
Index	152

About the Authors

Kerry Jacobs is Professor of Accounting at the University of New South Wales – Canberra. His research interests are focused on issues of public sector accountability, governance, audit, financial management and reform, particularly the relationship between accounting and politics. He received his PhD from the University of Edinburgh in Scotland and he has been honoured as a fellow of the New Zealand and the two Australian professional accounting associations. Kerry Jacobs has published over 40 and contributed to five different books about different aspects of public sector accountability and governance. He serves on the editorial board for a range of academic and professional journals on accounting and accountability and has provided international training and consulting in these areas.

Riccardo Pelizzo is a political scientist and a legislative studies specialist. He received a PhD (2004) in Political Science from the Johns Hopkins University in Baltimore. Riccardo Pelizzo has authored or edited more than ten books and is the author of more than 30 peer-reviewed articles. His work has been published or translated into ten languages (Arabic, Bahasa Indonesian, Chinese, English, French, German, Italian, Russian, Spanish and Vietnamese). He is a consultant on legislative affairs to the World Bank Institute.

Rick Stapenhurst is both a consultant and adviser to the World Bank Institute and a Professor of Practice at the Institute for the Study of International Development, McGill University. He has written extensively on issues related to anti-corruption and parliamentary strengthening; his most recent publications include *Parliamentary Oversight* (with Riccardo Pelizzo) and *African Parliamentary Reform* (with Andrew Imlach and Rasheed Draman). He has completed two Doctorates, one in Business and Commerce from Australian National University and the other in Business Administration from the International Graduate School.

Secretary-General's Foreword

The Statement of Purpose of the Commonwealth Parliamentary Association (CPA) provides that 'the CPA connects, develops, promotes and supports Parliamentarians and their staff to identify benchmarks of good governance and the implementation of the enduring values of the Commonwealth'.

The Association has carried out extensive work examining how Parliament manages public funds. To this end, a number of Study Groups, Workshops and Seminars have been convened to investigate Public Account Committees (PACs) and the role they play in parliamentary scrutiny and good governance. The work recognised that parliamentary effectiveness is dependent upon an active committee system which allows members to inquire into government administration and realise accountability.

Products of this practical work have been the production of two noteworthy publications. The first, *The Overseers: Public Accounts Committees and Public Spending*, published in 2002, gives an in-depth examination of the work and working practices of PACs. It highlights that strong parliamentary scrutiny regimes are an essential part of combating corruption and promoting good governance. The second, *The Budget Process*, took the role of Parliaments in financial scrutiny even further. Published in 2007, it gives an overview of the budget process and how Parliaments in diverse Commonwealth jurisdictions are developing practices and procedures to strengthen the effectiveness of this process.

Following on this work, and using the methodology employed previously, in 2012, the CPA and the World Bank Institute, with the support of the Legislative Assembly of British Columbia, convened a Study Group in Victoria, Canada. The mandate of the Study Group was to identify emerging patterns of the committee process as well as innovations to help PACs better respond to the challenges they face in safeguarding their contribution to financial scrutiny. It investigated the scarcity of research on new and evolving practices by Commonwealth and non-Commonwealth PACs on legislative oversight of the budget. The Study Group sought to enable Parliaments and development practitioners to make informed decisions on ways to improve Parliaments' audit performance. It allowed participating Parliaments to identify practical examples of good practice and provided direction on new avenues for inquiry. It also examined the progress made over the past decade in the work and functioning of PACs in the Commonwealth and beyond.

This Study Group added to the longstanding partnership between the CPA and the World Bank Institute aimed at strengthening parliamentary oversight and scrutiny.

This publication, *Following the Money*, is the end product of this Study Group. It addresses an aspect of the overall goal for parliamentary capacity building. The three authors, Riccardo Pelizzo, Rick Stapenhurst and Kerry Jacobs, formed the resource team together with Craig James, Clerk of the British Columbia Legislative Assembly. They supported the Study Group and were therefore a critical part of the deliberations made. These deliberations and the contributions of the participants are key to the content of the publication.

One of the Association's Strategic Objectives for 2013–17 is to assist members and branches to adopt good practice of democratic governance and to strengthen the institution of Parliament and the rule of law. It is our hope that this new publication will continue our work in this regard, not only for the members of our Commonwealth family but also in the wider global community.

The CPA is once again proud to join with the World Bank Institute and Pluto Press in publishing another instalment in the work towards improving parliamentary capacity for effective financial scrutiny.

Dr William F. Shija
Secretary-General
Commonwealth Parliamentary Association

Chairman's Foreword

Public Accounts Committees (PACs) are one of the central safeguards of parliamentary democracy. Within these committees, the full scale and breadth of government spending and revenue can be laid bare to scrutiny. Serving as a PAC member is one of the most demanding and rewarding responsibilities a Parliamentarian can benefit from during their career.

The Commonwealth Parliamentary Association (CPA) is committed to improving the accountability and transparency of Commonwealth governments through supporting and developing the skills of PAC members and parliamentary support staff. Through encouraging the intensive interrogation of the annual budget process, suggesting appropriate terms of reference for each context and technical financial training for committee members, the CPA is faithful to its raison d'être of supporting the advancement of parliamentary democracy. The variety of PAC conventions and practices which exists across the Commonwealth, as well as the common principles, confers a central role on the CPA in promoting best practice and benchmarks for others to consider.

Increasing the depth and scope of PAC work is congruent with the core values and fundamental principles represented within the Commonwealth Charter. The Charter will be used for many years by Commonwealth citizens as a benchmark to measure and reflect on the choices made by governments in their name. Commonwealth citizens look to the members of PACs to interrogate the decisions that are made on their behalf, publicising and highlighting where governments have fallen short and celebrating worthwhile and well managed public projects.

Eradicating corruption and misuse of public funds continues to be a key challenge for many parliamentarians across the Commonwealth. A strong PAC – in co-ordination with an effective and impartial Supreme Audit Institution – can combat this trend and compel governments to use more accountable and transparent methods of financial reporting. It is heartening that PACs are generally becoming stronger with greater public support; in some countries they are even being celebrated by civil society organisations and in the media for their historic investigations and reports.

As well as ensuring transparent expenditure records are created and maintained, 'value for money' auditing is becoming a crucial component of a PAC's arsenal. Increasingly members are turning to performance auditing to provide a more accurate picture of where improvements can be made. Another innovation has resulted in some PACs conducting ex ante scrutiny at the budget-setting stage, as well as ex post scrutiny when budgets have been spent. Thus the remit of a PAC is ever-expanding: the CPA seeks to assist members with tools and techniques to deliver the best from their committee deliberations.

These areas are where the CPA is helping build the capacity of PAC members and staff and promoting best practice. Routinely workshops and seminars are convened across the Commonwealth for members and staff to share expertise, knowledge and innovations in PAC procedure as well as providing an unparalleled opportunity for members to seek solutions through dialogue with experienced colleagues from similar and dissimilar contexts.

The CPA will continue in its efforts to assist and promote the work of PACs as part of its overarching endeavour, reinforcing parliamentary democracy across the Commonwealth.

Rt Hon. Sir Alan Haselhurst, MP
Chairman
Commonwealth Parliamentary Association

Preface

This book is intended to provide guidance and insight to those interested in or involved in the complex, diverse, and is rapidly changing world of Public Accounts Committees (PACs) and parliamentary oversight. In spite of complexity, diversity and transformations, PACs play a critical role in keeping governments accountable, promoting good governance, and creating the conditions for sustainable development. Therefore understanding and enhancing best practice has enormous significance.

This book presents a great wealth of insight into how PACs are organised, how they are empowered, and what they do. It also formulates clear recommendations as to how PACs could do better what they are mandated to do. The data presented and discussed in this book were collected with the help of the Commonwealth Parliamentary Association and the World Bank Institute. These two bodies commissioned this study, were actively involved in the data collection process, organised a Study Group and provided constant support to the authors.

Meetings of the Study Group were held in the Legislative Building of the Legislative Assembly of British Columbia in Victoria. We wish to extend our thanks to Mr Craig James and his staff for their warm hospitality and assistance.

This book is based on the survey data and on the insights gathered in the course of the Study Group. We hope it will be a valuable document for all those who wish to keep their government accountable, make parliamentary institutions work effectively and gain citizen trust.

Rick Stapenhurst
Riccardo Pelizzo
Kerry Jacobs

1
Introduction

There has been growing interest in processes of parliamentary accountability and oversight, which can be seen as part of the wider concern for reducing corruption and the reawakening of academic interest in political institutions and structures. At the centre of this trend has been the interest in the nature and operation of parliamentary Public Accounts Committees (PACs), particularly how to improve their capacity and performance. This is important because, despite the reduction in other aspects of public sector capacity and accountability, PACs have the ability to act in the public interest and independently from the executive[1] (Jones and Jacobs, 2006, p. 74).

In 2002, David McGee wrote a comprehensive report on two important elements in the system of public financial accountability; namely, the office of the Auditor-General, and the parliamentary oversight committee commonly referred to as the PAC (McGee, 2002). Based on the deliberations of a Study Group organised by the Commonwealth Parliamentary Association (CPA) in collaboration with the World Bank Institute (WBI) that the Ontario Legislature (Canada) hosted in 1999, he examined current practice in the Commonwealth regarding the roles and functions of Auditors-General and PACs, and the interaction between these two institutions. Chapter 2 reviews these findings. McGee (2002, p. 6) highlighted the importance of building the capacity of PACs

---

1. In this book, we use the terms 'executive' and 'government' interchangeably, to mean the executive arm of government.

and Auditors-General as a key priority for action. Other priority actions, such as ensuring both the PAC's and Auditor-General's independence from executive interference, and enhancing information exchange between PACs, can also be seen as a way of building and enhancing the capacity of these oversight institutions.

Subsequently, Stapenhurst et al. (2005) defined successful PAC performance and identified those factors that facilitate or hinder such successful performance. Using data that the WBI collected in 2002, Stapenhurst et al. (2005) analysed PAC practices and procedures in Commonwealth parliaments in Asia, Australasia, Canada, and the United Kingdom. Their findings were, to a considerable extent, consistent with McGee's conclusions. The PAC Chairs reported that information availability and bipartisanship/non-partisanship are critical conditions for a PAC's success, which two of McGee's three conclusions had previously suggested. However, Stapenhurst et al.'s analyses developed a much better understanding of how a PAC's capacity can be built. Two sets of factors seemed important in this regard: the PAC's institutional design, and its behaviour and functioning.

Stapenhurst et al. (2005) found that a PAC's success depended on how its power and mandate were *institutionalised.* In this respect, they suggested that PACs should focus on government financial activity and accountability rather than government policies. Second, they suggested that PACs should have the power to investigate all past and present government expenses, regardless of when they were made. They also suggested that PACs should be given the power to check whether government has actually undertaken steps to implement recommendations from the PAC itself and that PACs should have a close working relationship with the Auditors-General.

Stapenhurst et al. (2005) also found that a PAC's success depended on the behaviour of its members and the functioning of the committee itself. Here the authors identified some obvious best practices: PAC members should act in a non-partisan fashion and try to have a good working relationship with the other committee members despite possible political differences. In its functioning, the PAC should always strive for consensus, a point McGee (2002) previously emphasised. Stapenhurst et al. (2005, p. 25) also found that PACs' effectiveness increases whenever committees 'study the documentation and prepare themselves before the PAC and that the PACs should keep the transcripts of their meetings, publish their conclusions and recommendations, and seek to involve the public and the media'.

Over the past ten years, scholars and practitioners alike have conducted additional studies. Some of these were country case studies, while others compared PACs in different countries; some employed qualitative methods, while others used quantitative methods; some focused on PACs' organisation and structure, while others focused on their working practices. However, regardless of their approach, focus, and sample size, nearly all of these studies were concerned with what makes PACs work effectively or successfully. While this focus was nearly unanimous, there was much less agreement on what is responsible for PAC success or on how PAC success should be measured.

These studies used various indicators to measure success. Some studies measured success based on the amount of activities that PACs undertook, others did so based on PACs' ability to achieve policy-relevant results, to recover misallocated funds, or to save public money. And, of course, if one were to measure the success not so much of specific PACs but of the PAC as an institutional model or institutional archetype, then one could measure the success of the PAC based on its geographical reach. Contrary to popular belief, the first PAC was introduced in Denmark (see Box 7.1 in Chapter 7). However, the archetypal PAC was introduced a decade later in the United Kingdom and subsequently spread to all countries that were open to British political and institutional influence. More recently, countries that do not have historical or institutional ties with the Westminster model of parliamentary governance have adopted PACs. (Counterfactually, if institutional reformers in highly diverse countries such as Ethiopia, Indonesia, and Thailand had not regarded the PAC as an effective oversight tool, they would not have reformed their institutional architectures and their parliamentary committees by adopting it and adapting it to their needs.) Whether PAC success should be equated and possibly reduced to the amount of activities a PAC performs, to its ability to achieve policy-relevant results, and/or to recover misallocated funds or to save taxpayers' money is a question that this book addresses later on.

In this book, we highlight some of the developments regarding PACs over the past decade. Using data collected by the WBI in 2009–12, and information gathered by a second CPA-WBI Study Group that the Legislature of British Columbia hosted in 2012, we examine three principal developments. Following a review of McGee's (2002) seminal findings, in Chapters 3 and 4, we update previous analyses of PACs and, in particular, consider their structure, activities, and capacity. Importantly, it had long been postulated that PACs make a difference: when PACs are established and are effective, economic growth increases and corruption decreases. Our analyses confirm this – PACs do make a difference. Second, we examine PACs' capacity and performance in Chapter 5. In Chapter 6, we examine particular issues facing PACs in developing countries and smaller Parliaments, and, in Chapter 7, we consider the development of PACs in non-Commonwealth countries (i.e., those that do not have a 'Westminster parliamentary tradition') and look at an important but heretofore neglected issue – the adoption of 'ad hoc' PACs by military or authoritarian governments in the absence of a functioning parliament. In Chapter 8, we advance the theoretical claim, supported by our own data analyses and a large scholarly literature, that oversight effectiveness depends above all on the political will of the overseers. In this chapter, in addition to discussing why political will matters, we also discuss how such political will can be engendered and sustained. We conclude, in Chapter 9, by pulling the analyses together and proposing a 'good practice guide' based on the empirical analyses contained in this book. In the Appendix, we present a theoretical construct that places PACs in the broader constellation of legislative oversight tools and contextual factors.

In the remainder of this chapter, we present a general concept of public financial accountability. We underline the critical role that PACs play, noting their origin in the nineteenth century and their widespread use throughout the Commonwealth and elsewhere.

LEGISLATURES AND PUBLIC FINANCIAL ACCOUNTABILITY

In this section, we consider the role of the legislature in public financial accountability, and the concept of public financial accountability.

Role of the Legislature

Legislatures perform three functions – representative, legislative, and oversight (Sartori, 1987; Pasquino and Pelizzo, 2006). They perform a representative function in that they represent the will of the people, which is the legitimate source of authority in democratic countries. They perform a legislative function because, in addition to introducing legislation on their own, they have the power to amend, approve, or reject government bills. And they perform an oversight function by ensuring that governments implement policies and programmes in accordance with the wishes and intent of the legislature. They undertake this oversight function in two ways (Maffio, 2002): they oversee the preparation of a given policy (ex ante oversight), or they oversee the execution and the implementation of a given policy (ex post oversight).

Though most legislatures have the power to keep governments accountable for their actions and its policies, there is considerable variation in the legislative tools that legislatures can employ to perform their oversight function. This variation reflects to a large extent differences in the form of government and other constitutional arrangements. These tools include parliamentary committees, questions in the legislature, interpellations, debates, the estimates process, scrutiny of delegated legislation, private members' motions and adjournment debates that allow legislators to raise issues relating to the use or proposed use of governmental power. Other tools include calling on the government to explain actions it has taken, and requiring it to defend and justify its policies or administrative decisions (Pelizzo and Stapenhurst, 2004a, 2004b).

One of the tools that a legislature can use to further enhance oversight of the financial operations of government is a specialised committee. As noted above, in the 'Westminster model' of democracy (Lijphart, 1999), this committee is known as the PAC. The PAC is the 'audit committee' of Parliament and, as such, is the core institution of public financial accountability. As Frantzich (1979) pointed out, legislatures need useful information to perform their representative, legislative, and oversight function effectively. PACs, like legislatures and legislative committees, need information to perform their task effectively. This information is generally provided by the legislative auditor, or Auditor-General. In the Westminster model, the auditor reports to the legislature (and the public at large) on whether public sector resources are appropriately managed and accounted for by the executive government, and PACs use his/her reports as the cornerstone of their work.

Concept of Public Financial Accountability

Following implementation of a government's budget, the legislative auditor audits government accounts, financial statements, and operations – an oversight activity that may include value-for-money and performance auditing, and financial or compliance auditing. In most countries, this audit is followed by the consideration of the audit findings by the legislature. Where the legislatures' role in the budget process is effective, their deliberations on audit findings results in recommendations to the executive, which are reflected in future budgets and allow for continuous improvements in public financial accountability (see Figure 1.1).

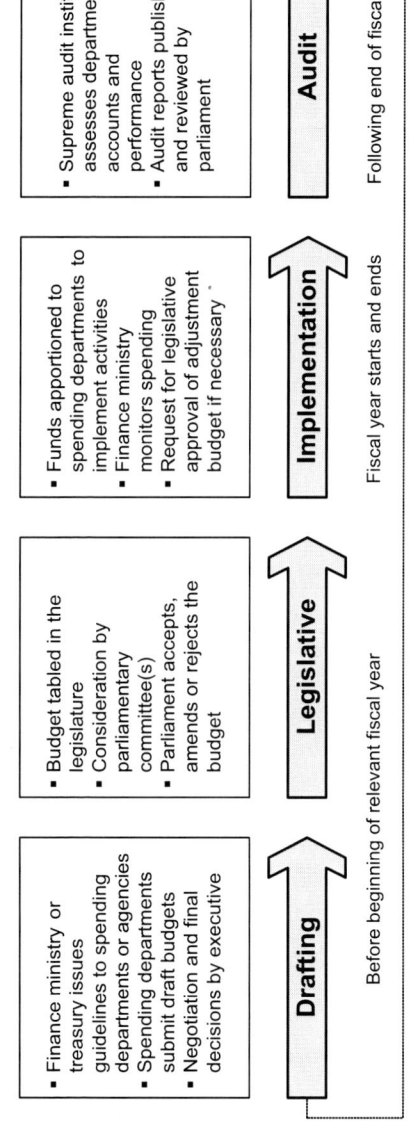

Figure 1.1: Stages of the annual budget process
Source: Wehner (2004).

The exact nature of the relationship and interaction between the legislature and the auditor depends, at least in part, on the model of the legislative auditor and the reporting relationship to the legislature. In most Commonwealth countries, the legislative auditor is the Auditor-General, whose office is a core element of parliamentary oversight. He/she reports directly to Parliament and the PAC. In some instances, the auditor is an Officer of Parliament, which guarantees his/her independence from the executive (as in Australia and the United Kingdom), while, in some other instances, he/she is independent of both the executive and the legislature (as in India). PACs are seen as the apex for financial scrutiny and have been promoted as a crucial mechanism to facilitate transparency in government financial operations (see Figure 1.2).

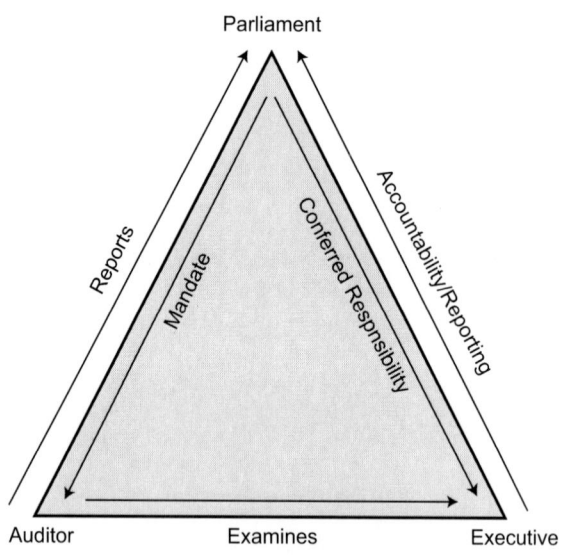

Figure 1.2: Fiduciary obligation

While the first PAC was constituted in Denmark in 1849, the archetypal PAC is associated with the model that originated in the nineteenth-century British Parliament. In Britain, the House of Commons had wrested control of finance from the Crown by the seventeenth century (Chubb 1952).[2]

However, it was in the nineteenth century that control was more developed. Chubb (1952, p. 28) tells the story of how the actions of Sir Francis Baring, a tireless critic of existing audit and accountability practices and an advocate for better parliamentary oversight of spending (UK House of Commons Debate, 9 August 1860, vol 160 cc 940–5), led to the establishment of a Standing Committee of Public Accounts. Baring's example of this accountability failure related to £80,000 that was voted for the Duke of Wellington's funeral and was drawn from the Exchequer by 5 April 1853. However, £24,000 was not spent on the funeral and, in 1856, the Pay Office was using it as a float for a system of payments and repayments for Army, Navy, and 'other requirements'. Baring argued that that was 'most confusing and unsatisfactory' because the money 'remained unaccounted for from 1853 to 1856, and had been applied to purposes which the House had no cognizance' (UK House of Commons Debate, 9 August 1860, vol 160 cc 940–5). Therefore, there was a need for better audit and oversight of all public monies. This committee was established in 1862 (UK House of Commons Debate, 3 April 1962, vol 166 cc 528–31) by William Gladstone (who had become Chancellor of the Exchequer in 1859). Gladstone's proposal for membership to the Committee of Public

2. However, this ignores the various commissions and select committees which were established in the UK as early as 1786 and the French Court of Audit (Cour des Comptes) which was re-established by Napoleon in September 1807. However, the Court of Audit was the successor to the Chamber of Accounts of Paris which began in 1303 and this was preceded by earlier forms of public accountability for funds associated with French practices of financial oversight and review first being associated with the ordinance of King Philip II in 1190 (www.ccomptes.fr). The debates about the formation of the UK Public Accounts Committee indicate that they were well aware of the French Court of Audit (Chubb, 1952, p. 26). The irony is that while the establishment of the 1861 PAC was informed by the practice of the French Court of Audit, the Court of Audit has strong parallels to what was known as the Exchequer Court, concerned with the King's Revenue in England, Ireland and Scotland. In that sense there has been some oversight of public funds in the UK since 1176, not long after the earliest Parliament was formed in England in 1066.

Accounts in 1862 primarily reflected the knowledge and expertise of the members (UK House of Commons Debate, 3 April 1862, vol 166 cc 528–31). In effect, a core requirement for the capacity of public accounts members is a sound understanding of public sector financial management and accountability.

Even though PACs have a common origin in the British PAC, there is considerable variation in their terms of reference and modus operandi across the Commonwealth and, indeed, in non-Commonwealth countries, too. In some instances, for example, the terms of reference are narrowly defined; in these cases, PACs concentrate exclusively on financial probity. In other instances, the terms of reference are more widely defined. Here, the committee does not simply focus on financial probity but also on the efficiency and effectiveness of programmes in achieving the objectives for which they were established. (Indeed, our findings indicate that this 'scope of work' is one of the principal factors affecting PAC performance.) There is considerable variation, too, regarding the relationship between the Auditor-General and the PAC, the status of the PAC in Parliament, how the PAC conducts its business, PAC reporting to the legislature, and requirements for government follow-up on PAC recommendations. McGee (2002) examines these and related issues in detail. An important feature in virtually all jurisdictions is the fact that PACs do not question the desirability of a particular policy – that is the mandate of parliamentary departmental committees; rather, PACs examine the efficiency and effectiveness in the *implementation* of policy.

In many countries, the Chair of the PAC is a prominent member of the opposition. This suggests two basic functions: first, it rebalances the power between the government and the opposition, and, second, it performs a symbolic function – it indicates the willingness of both the majority and the minority to operate, within the PAC, in a bipartisan manner. In some countries, such as the United Kingdom and India, this is result of 'a very strong convention' (McGee, 2002, p. 66). In other countries, this practice is codified by the same norms and rules that establish the PAC itself. For example, the article 120E(4) of the Standing Orders of Malta's Parliament establishes 'one of the members nominated by the Leader of the Opposition and so designated by him in consultation with the Leader of the House shall be appointed as Chairman of the Public Accounts Committee'. In a similar vein, art. 87(5) of the Standing Orders of the Tanzanian Parliament establish that 'the Chairperson for the Public Account Committee shall be elected from amongst the Members of the Committee from the Opposition'.

Australia represents an interesting exception to this general trend. In Australia, the Chair of the PAC is generally an MP from the parliamentary majority. This choice is defended with the argument that 'in Australia it is considered advantageous to have a government Member as Chair, as this can assist with the implementation of the PAC's recommendations. It is regarded as the duty of the Chair to advocate that the PAC's recommendations be taken up and implemented by the government. This can involve behind-the-scenes work persuading reluctant ministers to act. A government Member can do this more effectively than an opposition Member who as political opponent will not have the confidence of the ministers' (McGee, 2002, p. 66).

There is also some variation in the PAC's *terms of reference*. In some instances, for example, the terms of reference are narrowly defined; in these cases, PACs concentrate exclusively on financial probity. In other instances, the terms of reference are more widely defined. In some countries, the committee does not simply focus on financial probity but also on the efficiency and effectiveness of programmes in achieving the objectives for which they had been established. A PAC has, like any other standing committee, the power to investigate and examine all the issues that are referred to it by the parliament. The PAC can also investigate some specific issues such as the government's accountability to the Parliament with regard to the expenses approved by the government, the effectiveness and the efficiency of the policies enacted by the government, and the quality of the administration.

There is considerable variation also with regard to the relationship between the Auditor-General and the PAC, the status of the PAC in Parliament, the way in which the PAC conducts its business and reports to the legislature, and the requirements for government follow-up on PAC recommendations.

Depending on the scope of their mandate, PACs may be given additional and more-specific powers to perform their tasks. For example, they may be given the power to examine the public accounts, the comments on the public accounts, and all the reports drafted by the Auditor-General and by the National Audit Office. The PAC may also have the power to conduct, directly or indirectly, some investigations; to receive all the documentation that it considers necessary; to invite government members to attend the meetings of the PAC and to respond the questions of the PAC's members; to give publicity to their own conclusions; to report to Parliament; and to suggest to government, when this is considered necessary, how to modify its course of action.

The *size* of the PAC also varies from country to country. There are seven members in Malta, seventeen in Canada, and twenty-two in India. Interestingly, and in spite of the size of the membership, the distribution of seats in the PAC corresponds, as much as possible, to the distribution of seats in the whole assembly. This means that the government (or the government coalition) controls a majority of the PAC's seats.

Yet, what factors are responsible for the success of the PACs in performing their activities? Under what circumstances are PACs more likely to be effective? And, more importantly, in what respect are PACs effective? What kind of results can PACs effectively achieve? Neither McGee (2002) nor Stapenhurst et al. (2005) adequately address these questions, a shortfall this book addresses.

SOME ADDITIONAL COMMENTS AND OBSERVATIONS

A problem impinging on the effectiveness of many PACs is the fact that governments have sometimes little interest (if not open aversion) in the parliamentary oversight of their activities. Sometimes governments consider parliamentary oversight as an improper intrusion in their own sphere of influence, while, at other times, governments (and their members) think that PACs are not sufficiently informed or competent to formulate suggestions, criticisms, and observations worthy of their attention. These are serious problems because they indicate a poor understanding of the functions that executives and legislatures perform in parliamentary systems.

In parliamentary systems, the government has to govern and the Parliament has to check whether the government is governing well. When governments try to avoid parliamentary controls or when governments consider parliamentary controls as mere obstacles for the effectiveness of the government action, governments have a rather imperfect understanding of the principle of accountability.

This being said, it is important to keep in mind that this imperfect understanding represents a problem not only in newly established democracies, or in democratising regimes, which have, by definition, a fairly limited experience in the functioning of democratic institutions, but also in established and consolidated democracies. The Australian case is, in this respect, rather emblematic. Between 1932 and 1951, the PAC of the Australian Parliament never met because the government, which could not see which benefits were evolving from the meetings of this committee, decided that the meetings of this committee were not necessary. This is an important problem that can be solved only by inducing governments to be respectful of PACs and their activities.

Finally, the sound functioning of the PAC is seriously threatened (and possibly compromised) in countries in which corruption and other forms of improper behaviour (such as a conflict of interest) are tolerated. In fact, if there is no demand of good governance – of efficient, effective, transparent, and honest governance – by the civil society, the political class does not have any incentive to use the oversight mechanisms to check and possibly improve the quality of governance.

RECOMMENDED GOOD PRACTICES

Chapter 9 presents recommended benchmarks (or attributes) and key additional considerations (summarised here in Box 1.1). These are based on the empirical analyses contained in this book, and they extend and update the earlier work by Stapenhurst et al. (2005), Ngozwana (2009), and other sources. They also include comments from the Study Group.

Box 1.1: PAC benchmarks

Mandate and Powers
- There is clarity on the committee's role and responsibilities.
- The Rules and Acts of Parliament must empower the PAC with appropriate powers to carry out its mandate.
- PAC members should have a common understanding and articulation of the PAC's mandate, roles and powers.
- PAC members must have a good understanding of how PAC powers should be applied.
- The Rules and Acts of Parliament should allow for regular review and updating of PACs' mandate to ensure that it remains adequate and relevant to the current political and legislative context.
- The committee should have unconditional access to all government agencies and have the power to 'follow' government money provided to non-government service providers.
- In addition to issues raised by the Auditor, the committee has the power to investigate other matters.
- In smaller jurisdictions, there may be benefit in combining ex post and ex ante budget review within the remit of the PAC.
- The committee issues formal substantive reports to Parliament at least annually.
- Parliaments hold an annual debate on the work of the committee.
- The committee has established a procedure with the government for following up its recommendations and is informed about what, if any, action has been taken. ▶

Relationship with the Auditor-General
- The Auditor's Report is automatically referred to the committee and the Auditor meets with the committee to go over the highlights of the report.
- In all its deliberations, the committee uses the Auditor as an expert adviser.

Structure and Organisation
- The committee is small; committees seem to work well with five to eleven members, none of whom should be government ministers.

Some practical issues to consider in determining the size of a PAC:
- The PAC's mandate and responsibilities,
- The size of Parliament, and
- The number of audit reports to be reviewed by the PAC.

Political Representation
- Senior opposition figures are associated with the PAC's work, and probably chair the committee.
- The Chair is a senior parliamentarian, fair minded, and respected by Parliament.
- Committee membership should provide for adequate participation by opposition MPs; their proportion of PAC membership should at least represent their proportion of the seats in Parliament.
- A PAC should develop a clear written statement describing the role and responsibilities of a Chair.
- A PAC should consider developing a performance contract for the Chair, with clearly stated objectives, outputs, and performance indicators.

Term of Office
- The Committee is appointed for the full term of the Parliament.
- Experience and continuity are some of the critical factors for success of a PAC.

- The nature of a PAC's work is such that it may carry over from one year to another and may require follow up.
- A PAC invests resources in building capacity of members. The return on investment takes a substantial period to be realised.

Activities
- The committee meets frequently and regularly.
- The typical witness is a senior public servant (the 'accounting officer') accompanied by the officials who have detailed understanding of the issues under examination.
- A steering committee plans the committee's work in advance and prepares an agenda for each meeting to the full committee.
- The committee strives for some consensus in its reports.
- Hearings are open to the public; a full verbatim transcript and summary minutes are quickly available for public distribution.

Performance
- A committee should assess its performance annually.
- A committee should have a performance framework to assess its effectiveness/performance.

Resources
- Committees should be involved in determining their own budgets. Such budgets should provide financial resources for member allowances, site visits, and costs related to public hearings.
- The committee is adequately staffed, with an experienced clerk and a competent researcher(s).
- Specialised training (including orientation and mentoring) should be provided to new PAC members.

BIBLIOGRAPHY

Chubb, B. 1952. *The Control of Public Expenditure*, Oxford University Press, Oxford.

Frantzich, S. E. 1979. 'Computerized Information Technology in the US House of Representatives', *Legislative Studies Quarterly*, vol. 4, no. 2, pp. 255–80.

Lijphart, A. 1999. *Patterns of Democracy*, Yale University Press, New Haven.

McGee, D. 2002. *The Overseers: Public Accounts Committees and Public Spending*, Commonwealth Parliamentary Association and Pluto Press, London.

Maffio, R. 2002. 'Quis custodiet ipsos custodes? Il controllo parlamentare dell'attività di governo in prospettiva comparata', *Quaderni di Scienza Politica*, vol. IX, no. 2, pp. 333–83.

Malhotra, S. G. C. 2000. 'Ensuring Executive Accountability: India's Public Accounts Committee', *The Parliamentarian*, pp. 179–86.

Miller, R., Pelizzo, R. and Stapenhurst, F. 2004. 'Parliamentary Libraries, Institutes and Offices – The Sources of Parliamentary Information', WBI Working Paper, World Bank Institute, Washington DC.

Pasquino, G. and Pelizzo, R. 2006. *Parlamenti Democratici*, Il Mulino, Bologna.

Pelizzo, R. and Stapenhurst, F. 2004a. 'Legislatures and Oversight: A Note', *Quaderni di Scienza Politica*, vol. XI, no. 1, pp. 175–88.

Pelizzo, R. and Stapenhurst, F. 2004b. 'Tools of Legislative Oversight', Policy Research Working Paper no. 3388, World Bank Institute, Washington DC.

Rockman, B. A. 1984. 'Legislative-Executive Relations and Legislative Oversight', *Legislative Studies Quarterly*, vol. 9, no. 3, pp. 387–440.

Sartori, G. 1987. *Elementi di teoria politica*, Il Mulino, Bologna.

SIGMA. 2002. 'Relations Between Supreme Audit Institutions and Parliamentary Committees', *Survey of Parliamentary and External Auditing Institutions in European Union Candidate Countries*. SIGMA paper no. 33, OECD and European Union.

Stapenhurst, R., Saghal, V., Woodley, W. and Pelizzo, R. 2005. 'Scrutinizing Public Expenditures. Assessing the Performance of Public Accounts Committees in Comparative Perspective', Policy Research Working Paper no. 3613, World Bank Institute, Washington DC.

University of Strathclyde. 1992. 'Teething the Watchdogs', *Report of a Panel Discussion Comparing US and United Kingdom Legislative Committees*, 1992.

Wehner, J. 2004. 'Back From the Sidelines? Redefining the Contribution of Legislatures to the Budget Cycle', World Bank Institute Working Paper, World Bank Institute, Washington DC.

2
Looking Backwards – McGee and the First CPA-WBI Study Group on Public Accounts Committees

Relatively little academic or practitioner attention has been devoted to the role of parliament in the review and control of public expenditure, despite the fact that the control of public finance is the historical heart of parliamentary constitutional pre-eminence. However, this changed in 2002 when David McGee[3] reported on a Study Group and a survey of the Public Accounts Committees (PACs) in Commonwealth countries. McGee's objective was not to engage in academic discussion, but to strengthen the work of these committees and thereby of Parliament by providing models of good governance (McGee, 2002, p. 1). As a practical document, McGee's (2002) book was brief and based on what existing PAC chairs felt were the critical success factors and best-practice for an effective PAC. It provided an important guide for Members of Parliament who found themselves on one of these committees, and was an important trigger for further study and analysis of the factors that did (or did not) underpin the effective parliamentary oversight of public finance.

3. At the time, Clerk of the New Zealand Parliament.

As Chapter 1 notes, the origins of McGee (2002) are in the work of the Commonwealth Parliamentary Association (CPA) and the World Bank Institute (WBI) and, more especially, in a Study Group on 'Parliamentary Committees: Enhancing Democratic Governance', which the Ontario Legislature hosted between 28 and the 31 May 1999. The Study Group comprised members and former members of Commonwealth PACs, observers and advisers from the CPA, the WBI, Auditors-General and Commonwealth bodies.

The topics covered by the Study Group during their deliberations were: (1) PACs in the Commonwealth; (2) the ecology of the PAC; (3) the committee's purpose, scope, and functions; (4) the structure of the PAC; (5) the relationship between the Auditor-General and the PAC; (6) special problems of PACs in small Parliaments; (7) methods of PAC committee operations; (8) the position of the PAC in the overall committee structure; and (9) the future of the PAC. The three main conclusions were that: (1) there is a need to build the capacity (through resourcing and training) of Parliaments, PACs, and Auditors-General to carry out their functions of oversight and governance; (2) it is critical that the independence of the Auditor-General from political or legal constraint be maintained, and (3) it is important that PACs develop the means to exchange information on developments, standards, and best practice. McGee recorded the Study Group's deliberations and, together with the findings of a questionnaire study of 70 CPA branches, this became the basis of McGee (2002).

PUBLIC ACCOUNTS COMMITTEE AS PART OF DEMOCRATIC ACCOUNTABILITY

McGee (2002) begins by observing that, while Commonwealth Members of Parliament (MPs) represent diverse cultures, they are united in their interest to promote democracy through parliamentary systems. However, despite diversity in structures and practices, the principle of the public control over spending is well established. Democracy requires accountability for the exercise of power, particularly accountability for the expenditure of public funds. Therefore, as a tool of financial accountability and oversight, the PAC represents an important way for parliaments to hold the executive branch of government to account for their operating policies, actions, and for their management and use of public resources.

The Study Group (McGee, 2002) argued that accountability was not just about avoiding illegal actions, but also required an ethos of compliance, efficiency, and good governance. This ethos was embodied in the work of the Auditor-General, which, while being a separate institution, was strongly intertwined with the work of the PAC. The Study Group believed that the PAC and the Auditor-General are essential joint elements of democratic accountability, while recognising the diversity in how these two institutions related in the countries studied and represented. The Study Group recommended that an Auditor-General should be recognised as an 'officer of the Parliament', or, where this is more appropriate, of the lower House of Parliament.

McGee (2002) traces the origins of the PAC back to 1861 when the UK House of Commons at Westminster established such a committee to consider the reports of the Controller and Auditor-General.[4] As Chapter 1 notes, the UK PAC was driven by the motivation to reduce corruption and waste and to maintain parliamentary sovereignty over funds (accountability), and the early work of both the PAC and the Auditor-General was to ensure that spending was properly authorised and to identify and eliminate waste. McGee (2002) claims that the major contemporary driver for PACs is the need to enhance international lending institutions' perception of national creditworthiness and governance. This is more than just a legitimacy argument because international financial assistance is often intermingled with a country's domestic revenues, and therefore the robustness of systems of public financial accounting and financial oversight become very important to a lending institution.

4. Although, as previously noted, the first modern PAC was established in Denmark in 1849.

AUDITORS-GENERAL

McGee (2002) and the Study Group spent a considerable amount of time discussing the position and work of Auditors-General. They felt that the key issue was the independence of the Auditor-General from the entity being audited, which was understood as independence from the government. However, the question of independence had a number of aspects such as appointment, tenure, career expectations, method of removal, funding, and legal immunity, all of which could enhance or undermine independence. Central to independence was that the Auditor-General be associated with the legislature as an Officer of Parliament rather than being part of the executive arm of government (as the 'government' auditor). They suggested that such status would clearly establish that the Auditor-General is responsible and accountable to Parliament rather than to government.

The Study Group highlighted processes that enhance consultation and therefore the legitimacy and independence of the Auditor-General, while recognising that there was not one 'correct' manner for the appointment of an Auditor-General. In Canada, nominations are made by a special committee of audit professionals (including the professional accounting bodies,) and the Chair of the PAC is consulted before the final nomination is made by Order in Council. The Study Group recommended that the agreement of (or at least a consultation with) the Chair of the PAC and other key stakeholders was good practice in Auditors-General appointments.

The Study Group recognised that there were a variety of lengths of Auditor-General service, but that a reasonable term of office is necessary in order to exercise the role of the Auditor-General. In Canada and Australia, the Auditor-General serves for ten years, while it is fifteen years in the United States. The Study Group did not recommend a specific term of office because they felt that the independence of the Auditor-General was related to the manner of Auditors-General appointment and the funding of the office rather than the term of service. There are national differences in allowing an extension of an Auditor-General's term of service: extensions are prohibited in the countries with a relatively long term of service but permitted in other jurisdictions. The Study Group suggested that the question of renewal depended on the country and the circumstances, and made no specific recommendations. However, the Study Group highlighted concerns around the rules for an Auditor-General's removal from office, and recommended that this should be clearly defined in law and should be comparable to the conditions for the removal of a judge.

The Study Group argued that the Auditor-General should have a professional relationship with the executive while maintaining independence, and that they should have a working relationship with every committee of the legislature and most particularly the PAC. The nature of the relationship between the Auditor-General and the PAC differs between jurisdictions. In some cases, the relationship is very close, with the PAC referring matters to the Auditor-General for report. In other settings, the relationship is more distant, with the Auditor-General only appearing to give evidence as a witness.

Historically, the work of an Auditor-General was focused on determining the probity of public spending and expressing an audit opinion on whether the financial statements fairly represented the financial transactions of government (financial audit) (Chubb, 1952). However, since the 1970s, there has been growth in value-for-money or efficiency audits that focus on the economy, efficiency, and effectiveness of government activity. The key issue is that, in their audit work (most particularly the performance audit work), Auditors-General do not question the merits of government policy objectives but rather only the implementation and delivery of that policy. The Study Group recognised the growth of performance audit work (together with the growth of cross-cutting work such as environmental and gender issues), but also noted that it has a greater potential to bring the auditor into conflict with government departments (and by extension the government).

The Study Group strongly defended the powers of an Auditor-General to inquire into any matter in their mandate. However, they also suggested that the Auditor-General should be open to suggestions from the PAC, other MPs, and the public on profitable areas for attention. In general, the Study Group endorsed a regular programme of consultation around the Auditor-General's work programme.

The issue of funding and resourcing is critical to the independence and to the proper functioning of an Auditor-General. The Study Group recommended that the PAC be briefed by the Auditor-General and the Treasury (or Finance Ministry) so they can form an opinion on the adequacy of the funding available to the Auditor-General. This was because a squeeze on funding could undermine the independence of the Auditor-General. The Study Group also felt that it was necessary for the Auditors-General and their staff to have an appropriate level of legal protection in order to do their work, particularly when they are faced with fraud and corruption.

The Study Group recognised that, in many countries, there has been considerable change in the nature and structure of public sector entities, which has resulted in a number of government entities being privatised. This privatisation process raises important issues about the extent of the Auditor-General's mandate. The Study Group argued that, despite privatisation, the Auditor-General should retain the power to follow public funds into the private sector and examine any company who receives public funds to deliver public services. This should also extend to reviewing outsourcing arrangements and any residual 'public service obligation' of privatised entities. The argument that some issues are 'commercial in confidence' because they relate to contractual arrangements should not be used as an excuse to limit parliamentary accountability for publicly funded services.

While the work of the Auditor-General needs to be reported to Parliament and the wider community, this does not eliminate the need to have the factual content of the report reviewed by the department or agency that is the subject of the report. In addition, any adverse conclusions or recommendations need to be disclosed in advance so that any department or official named is given a right of reply. While reporting to Parliament is a central responsibility of the Auditor-General, the Study Group also recommend that the Auditor considers the use of news media and devise a strategy (normally in partnership with a PAC) to ensure that their recommendations are addressed and followed up. In conclusion, they recommend that an Auditor-General devote some attention to monitoring and reviewing their own performance and impact.

The strong emphasis on the Auditor-General and the independence of the Auditor-General is not surprising when you consider that the work of 85 percent of the PACs surveyed was primarily dependent on the Auditor-General's report, and that, for 61 percent of the PACs, the timing of their examinations was governed by the tabling to the Auditor-General's report. The practice and work of these PACs were dominated by their focus on the Auditor-General's reports, and there was comparatively little work that was self-initiated or initiated by other sources such as Parliament or the public.

PUBLIC ACCOUNTS COMMITTEES

McGee (2002) restates the notion that the first PAC was established in 1861 in the UK House of Commons. While this is not strictly true (as Chapter 1 shows, the first PAC was established in Denmark in 1849), it is clear that the British PAC became a powerful model that influenced the development across many Commonwealth and non-Commonwealth countries alike (Jacobs and Jones, 2009).

Terms of Reference

McGee (2002) acknowledged that the PAC is not the only parliamentary committee that exercises a financial oversight function: departmentally based committees may also perform this kind of role. The use of departmental or area specific committees might be particularly helpful if an area of inquiry is focused on evaluating policy (which is often outside of the rules or conventions governing PAC work) or if the area requires a particular specialist expertise.[5] In addition, the terms of reference of a PAC might be expressed narrowly in terms of financial probity and regularity or more broadly in terms of examining the effectiveness and efficiency of programmes. However, an important part of this mandate is to ensure the independence of the Auditor-General and to bolster the effectiveness of that office. Therefore, the work of the Auditor-General is seen as the staple of the PAC. In many jurisdictions (such as Australia), there is a statutory obligation to review all the reports of the Auditor-General that are tabled in Parliament. The Study Group suggested that this close link between the Auditor-General and the PAC was 'inevitable and desirable'. However, it was also important that a PAC has the ability (and capacity) to pursue matters of interest to members (or to the Parliament) that have not been the subject of an Auditor-General's report.

McGee (2002) outlines a 'terms of reference' for a PAC with the statement that 'PACs examine the Public Accounts, the Auditor General's Reports and matters relating to the effective and efficient use of money appropriated by Parliament'. In contrast, McGee (2002) suggests that issue of macro-economic policy, tax policy, the decision to borrow funds, and the examination of the government's budget estimates are beyond a PAC's mandate. This recommendation is interesting because, in many jurisdictions, the role of an estimates committee (charged with the examination of the budget) is combined with the role of a PAC. McGee's (2002) argument for the separation of these roles is because of the 'high policy' nature of the estimates. This is consistent with his position that the PAC should not be considering questions of policy. The merits or otherwise of combining the Public Accounts and the Estimates role requires further evaluation.

McGee's (2002) argues against a PAC considering issues of policy because considering policy issues makes it hard to maintain the unanimity conventions among members, and policy issues lead to more minority reports. Judgments on policy

---

5. PAC subcommittees were also seen as another way to address this kind of issue.

are likely to be contentious because they will tend to bring the committee into conflict with the government at a ministerial level, rather than focusing on the implementations of policy, which is a departmental issue. In addition, a consideration of policy will involve extending hearings beyond departmental witnesses to include a much broader group of people. However, it is also acknowledged that the line between policy and implementation is not always clear-cut because policies, such as outsourcing or privatisation, involve questions of policy and implementation. The recommendation of the Study Group was that the PAC should focus on calling departmental officials as witnesses rather than ministers as a strategy to keep the focus on administrative issues rather than policy ones. The survey suggested that around 30 percent of the PACs would call ministers to give evidence while around 70 percent would never call ministers.

Membership of PAC

McGee (2002) argues that the need to act with 'focus on accountability' rather than a more 'policy-orientated focus' and working towards bipartisan unanimity means that some members are reluctant to act on a PAC and that service on a PAC might be career-inhibiting rather than career-enhancing. Therefore, effort is needed to enhance the status of the PAC and to recognise the value of the PAC's work.

The survey of 70 CPA branches found that the typical PAC has 11 members. However, this was heavily biased because the average across the Asian Parliaments was 17 members, while the average for everywhere else was only 9 members (in the smaller Caribbean jurisdictions, the average was only 6 members). Generally, the party affiliation of the PAC's membership is proportionate to the party membership of the House. However, this poses difficulties where there is a domination of a single party in Parliament. McGee (2002) tells the story of one Parliament in Africa, where all the members of the PAC are from the government. Clearly, the question is whether this is because there are no opposition members in Parliament, or because the opposition members are excluded from the PAC. Singapore is an interesting example on this issue because all of the PAC members are often from the same political party. When one of the authors asked how they provoked debate and discussion within the PAC, it was suggested that some of the members are designated as 'opposition' and are asked to challenge the government's position.

McGee (2002) strongly emphasised involving senior opposition members with the work of the PAC, normally through the Chair role. In the survey, they found that two thirds of the cases had opposition Chairs, and this is a very strong convention in India and the UK. The alternative argument made by CPA members from jurisdictions with a government Chair was that a government Chair assists with the implementation of the PAC recommendations, which might be more problematic with an opposition chair. The Study Group argued that the capacity of the Chair to carry out the office was more critical than whether they came from the government or opposition ranks.

Given the skills required to craft bipartisan unanimity, and the potential career-limiting implications of a government Chair producing a report that challenged and embarrassed the government, the skills and capacity of a good Chair are most likely to be found in a very experienced parliamentarian. This is because the Chair cannot play an overly political role; he/she needs to be able to press ministers to have the committee recommendations implemented, work in co-operation with the bureaucracy, and act independently of party pressures. The survey found that the term of office and the chair and members is usually the same as the parliamentary session; however, there are a number of exceptions because some (such as one Canadian province) have no fixed term while other Parliaments (Zambia) require some members to leave the PAC each year.

The Study Group recognised that most of the members assigned to serve on a PAC will not necessarily have an existing knowledge of accountability issues in government or of the role of the PAC in reinforcing accountability. Therefore, there was a need to offer training and support for new and for existing PAC members. While further work was required to define the specific training needs of PAC members, the Study Group suggested that study should cover (1) reading and understanding public accounts, (2) familiarity with the structure of the government, (3) introduction to the work of the Auditor-General, and (4) reflection on their role as PAC members. The Study Group suggested that retired Chairs of PACs, Auditors-General, and universities could be potential sources of training for PAC members.

It is interesting to reflect that the key areas of knowledge reflected in (1) and (3) could be characterised as accounting knowledge. It is also important to note the emphasis that Gladstone placed on 'talent, knowledge, and experience' in public accounts and in control of public monies as the criteria for membership of the earliest Westminster PACs (Chubb, 1952, p. 37). While the statement by Ben Chifley (Australia's 16th Prime Minister from 1945 to 1949) that 'only accountants would be qualified to be members' of a PAC (Australian Commonwealth Parliamentary Debates, 10 March 1949, p. 769, Jones and Jacobs, 2012) is somewhat excessive, it is questionable how members can be expected to fulfil the mandate of a PAC to 'examine the Public Accounts, the Auditor General's Reports and matters relating to the effective and efficient use of money appropriated by Parliament' (McGee, 2002, p. 58) without some knowledge and experience of accounting. Perhaps the tendency noted by McGee (2002) for PAC members to stray away from issues of accountability and financial oversight and into issues of policy is evidence of a need for further training in this area.

Second only to training and experience is the issue of resourcing. The Study Group found that the resources provided to PACs varied considerably between different countries: India, for instance, had 22 staff and a dedicated library, while some small or developing countries had no staff resources at all. It is suggested that the staff of the Auditor-General's office or staff from the Treasury may be able to assist the PAC in these kinds of settings; however, this can also cause some conflict-of-interest issues. It is also suggested that universities might be able to provide assistance and support. Adequate resourcing, funding, and staffing is necessary if the PAC is to fulfil its mandate.

Working Practices

PACs work in a variety of ways. Some PACs are inactive and never meet at all; others meet once or twice a year, and others meet as often as twice a week while Parliament is in session. McGee (2002) argues that committees that meet on a frequent basis have a better opportunity to promote consensual working practices and endorse regular meetings, while recognising that this is a function of the institutional context.

Historically, PACs have not sought publicity and have tended to conduct their meetings privately to support consensual working practices. However, there was a move to conduct hearings more publicly in order to improve public recognition and understand of the need for accountability. Fifty-five percent of respondents indicated that hearings were now open to the public and to the media, and they did not report that this more open approach has negatively impacted their working practice. Therefore, the Study Group was supportive of open hearings where there are no specific security or confidential implications.

From a practical perspective, the Study Group recognised that some PACs utilise subcommittees to fulfil their work, and suggested that this might be helpful in some settings. The Study Group observed that the majority of witnesses called to a hearing are departmental officials, and warned against calling ministers because of the danger of getting embroiled in policy debates. They also suggested that PACs do not take individual complaints and allegations of improper or unfair treatment, which should be referred to the Ombudsman or a minister of the government, but that the PAC should focus on systemic rather than individual issues.

There was considerable diversity in PAC reporting practices with some only reporting once a year (or once a parliamentary session) and others reporting more often. In the survey, 17 percent of the PACs indicated that they reported once a parliamentary session or once a year, while 53 percent of PACs indicated that they reported when they determined (but usually at the end of the investigation). However, it is unclear how often 'as the committee determined' actually is. The Study Group supported the notion that PACs should regularly report to Parliament and these reports should be publicly available. Eighty-seven percent of the PACs surveyed noted that their reports were publicly available, with only 13 percent noting that they weren't publicly available.

There was some debate around the impact of PAC findings on individual public servants. The Study Group recommended that evidence of fraud or corruption be passed on to the competent prosecuting authority rather than risk the possibility that a PAC investigation could prejudice a successful legal prosecution. However, where there is evidence of misconduct which, while not being criminal, fell below the standard expected, there were alternative views over the appropriate action. One group felt that responsibility is too easily avoided and that disciplinary powers over officials is justified, including the kind of fines and legal punishment powers held by the French Court of Audit. The other perspective was that the PAC did not have the responsibility to fix individual responsibility or to impose penalties and that this role rested with the government. The Study Group did not resolve this disagreement, suggesting that the relationship between the PAC and the bureaucracy depends on local circumstances. However, the clear opinion was that the recommendations of PAC reports are made to government and that it is government who is obliged to deal with a problem revealed by a PAC inquiry. It was also recognised that PAC reports are inevitably focused on past performance. This can be a problem because the issues identified in a report might already have been resolved. While the Study Group (McGee, 2002, p. 78) raised the possibility of reviewing programmes as they are implemented, they also suggested that lessons should be drawn from the retrospective reports to improve the delivery of programmes and public sector financial management. The implication of this recommendation is that PAC reports must go beyond the descriptive analysis to identify and highlight these broader lessons.

It is critical that there be an effective response, and hopefully implementation, of PAC recommendations. Most Parliaments require that governments respond in a certain timeframe to PAC recommendations, and the acceptance rate to the recommendations are relatively high.[6] Some Parliaments (but not all) will debate in the house the PAC reports and the government responses. The recommendation is that parliamentary debate, at least on an annual basis, is essential. In addition, to debate, it is critical that there is a follow-up of the implementation of the government responses to PAC recommendations. In some settings, this is done by the Auditor-General, who follows up the implementation of both their recommendations and the recommendations of the PAC. However, the Study Group did not specifically recommend this.

PROBLEMS FOR DEVELOPING AND SMALLER PARLIAMENTS

The Study Group recognised that PACs in smaller Parliaments or in developing countries faced particular challenges. While these groups were not exactly the same, both can suffer from a lack of resources and a lack of expertise. In addition, a problem for smaller parliaments is the difficulties in finding members to serve on the PAC (given a limited number of members and the commitment to other committees) and the difficulties in getting members to attend PAC meetings. One suggestion for small bicameral parliaments is to pool membership across both houses and form a joint committee. This also seems to be a successful approach in some larger jurisdictions. The doctrine of not including ministers

---

6. The reported survey response in this area makes no sense because McGee (2002, p. 101) suggests that the executive is required to respond to PAC recommendations in 8 percent of jurisdictions and is not required to respond in 20 percent. We would suggest that this was most likely a typographic error and 80 percent of the jurisdictions studied are required to respond.

in a PAC may also pose problems in finding sufficient government members to serve on a PAC in small Parliaments. One suggestion is to co-opt non-Members of Parliament as non-voting members of the PAC. (This may be an effective way to enhance the skills and expertise of the PAC and is consistent with the Danish PAC model, where currently only half of the PAC members are MPs.) It is also recognised that, for some small or developing jurisdictions, the Auditor-General (where sufficiently resourced) can play an important secretariat role for the PAC. In closing, the Study Group suggested that the lack of legal protection for the Auditor-General and the lack of public and parliamentary understanding of the role of the PAC is a particular problem in developing countries. Finally, the solution to the problems of PACs in both developing and developed settings is the enhancement of information exchange between PACs in different jurisdictions and the development of handbooks, benchmarking, websites, and conferences.

CONCLUSIONS

The Study Group and the resulting McGee (2002) book was an enormously valuable contribution to our understanding of PACs around the world. While there were a few previous studies on PACs, these tended to focus on single jurisdictions or historical material. However, the primary value of McGee (2002) was as a practical handbook, guide, and initial training tool for MPs who found themselves on a PAC. One of the central challenges is the diversity revealed in McGee (2002). It is clear that there were a number of different ways to approach things, and it was far from clear what was best. It is also clear that the McGee (2002) study represents a highly normative set of statements of how PAC Chairs felt that PACs ought to function, which was heavily grounded in the ideal of the Westminster tradition. However, there is the possibility that deviation from this traditional ideal might actually lead to better performance. Therefore, questions remain about the relationship between some of the key recommendations found in

McGee (2002) and effective PAC performance, the relationship between PAC practice and underlying institutional structure in different Parliaments, and the possibility of a number of different 'best-practice types' emerging that fit the local conditions and needs in new and interesting ways. Chapters 3–6 further examine these issues.

BIBLIOGRAPHY

Chubb, B. 1952. *The Control of Public Expenditure*, Oxford University Press, Oxford.

Jones, K. and Jacobs, K. 2009. 'Legitimacy and Parliamentary Oversight in Australia: The Rise and Fall of Two Public Accounts Committees', *Accounting, Auditing & Accountability Journal*, vol. 22, issue 1, pp. 1 –34.

Jones, K. and Jacobs, K. 2012. 'The Cerberus from Warringah: F. A. Bland and the Renaissance of the Public Accounts Committee', *Working Paper Australian Catholic University*.

McGee, D. 2002. *The Overseers: Public Accounts Committees and Public Spending*, Commonwealth Parliamentary Association and Pluto Press, London.

Raynaud, J. 1988. *La Cour des comptes*, Presses Universitaires de France, Paris.

3
The Structure of Public Accounts Committees

INTRODUCTION

As Chapter 1 notes, David McGee's (2002) analysis of Public Accounts Committees (PACs) represented a turning point in the study of legislative oversight: it was the first comprehensive, global, comparative analysis of Public Accounts Committees. Building on the work of McGee, two major global surveys have been carried out over the past decade with the second (conducted in 2009) covering 58 national and sub-national PACs in Africa, Asia, Australia/New Zealand, Canada, the Caribbean, Europe, and the Pacific. This chapter analyses this more recent work and thereby provides an up-to-date overview of the structure of PACs around the world.

THE 'OLD STORY'

McGee's Assessment in the Late 1990s

McGee (2002) investigated several characteristics of PACs in order to provide a comprehensive and detailed overview of their work and, more importantly, because he believed that some

THE STRUCTURE OF PUBLIC ACCOUNTS COMMITTEES

characteristics could have a significant impact on the functioning and the success of committee. Here, we recap some of the issues presented in Chapter 2.

First, he underlined that the size of a legislature matters. He extensively discussed the importance of the size of a legislature and identified a legislature with 60 seats as the size under which a legislature may encounter difficulties in performing its tasks. The evidence, collected in a Commonwealth survey of PACs and in a Commonwealth Parliamentary Association (CPA)-World Bank Institute (WBI) Study Group, made it quite clear that, for committees operating in small legislatures, it is very difficult to be effective. In a small legislature, Parliamentarians may be required to serve on numerous committees; they thus face severe time constraints, which prevents them from adequately performing their PAC duties. Furthermore, in small legislatures 'there are inherent problems for a PAC because there may be a lack of government members to serve on the committee (and on parliamentary committees generally) given the large proportion of the members who will hold ministerial office' (McGee, 2002, p. 83).

A second, often related, factor is the size of the PAC itself. McGee (2002, p. 95) reported that the average size of a PAC is 11 members, that Asian PACs are usually larger (17 members on average), that Caribbean PACs are the smallest (6 members on average) and that 'the average for all regions of the Commonwealth, excluding Asia, is nine'. At one extreme, if a PAC is very small, its members may have too many additional committee appointments to do their job properly, to attend the PAC meetings, and to make meaningful contributions to the committee activities, while, if the PAC is very large, it may become unwieldy and difficult to chair and achieve a consensus.

McGee (2002) went on to argue that, while the unsuccessful performance of a small PAC can be attributed to its small size, the unsuccessful performance of larger PACs could be attributed to the lack of adequate resources, staff, and capacity. Hence, the second factor affecting the performance of PACs is the size of the staff at its disposal.

A third factor is represented by the adequate representation of opposition parties in the committee. McGee (2002, p. 61) reported that the balance of political power in a PAC usually reflects the balance of political power in the legislature as a whole, that government parties usually control a majority of seats on PACs, that 'a significant proportion of Parliaments have PACs which are not dominated by government Members' (McGee, 2002, p. 96), but that, in one African legislature, the government party controls all the seats on the PAC.[7] The problem can be particularly acute in small jurisdictions, where, because of the shortage of available members and the small size of the committee, opposition parties may not have adequate representation on the committee.

Finally, a key determinant of the success of PACs was considered to be the political affiliation of committee Chair. Specifically, McGee (2002) suggested that PACs chaired by an opposition MP are generally more successful than PACs chaired by MPs affiliated with the government majority. He noted that, globally, two thirds (67 percent) of PACs are chaired by an opposition member, but that there are also significant differences between the various regions. For example, while it is quite unlikely for a government MP to chair a PAC in Canada, the Caribbean, and the United Kingdom/Atlantic region, it is quite common in Australia, where 86 percent of the PACs are chaired by a government MP.

The World Bank Institute's First In-Depth Review

In 2002, the WBI surveyed 52 national and sub-national legislatures in Commonwealth countries in Asia, Australasia, Canada, and the United Kingdom.[8] The evidence generated by this survey

---

7. It is important to keep in mind that here McGee is making two different points: he is stating that government parties usually have more members serving on the PAC, but is also careful enough to point out that, in a large majority of PACs, opposition forces are also given adequate representation and that opposition forces are not greatly outnumbered by government MPs.
8. Of these 52 PACs, 28 operated at the sub-national level and 24 operated at the national level. An analysis of the 24 national PACs can be found in Pelizzo (2011).

was presented in a series of publications (Stapenhurst et al., 2005; Pelizzo et al., 2006; Pelizzo and Stapenhurst, 2007; Pelizzo, 2011) that evaluated and measured PAC success, identified success factors, and detected regional trends. They showed that 'success' is a multifaceted phenomenon, that PACs are more likely to succeed in some respects than in others, and that some structural conditions are important in ensuring the success of a PAC. The success factors were divided into three categories: formal powers, working practices, and the composition of the PAC, which corresponds broadly to the structural conditions identified by McGee. Using only national legislatures from a dataset that also provided information about sub-national legislatures,[9] Pelizzo (2011) measured the size of PACs, the representation of opposition MPs, the size of the staff, and the presence of opposition Chairs.

With regard to the size of a PAC, the results of the analyses were consistent with the findings presented by McGee. They revealed that the size of PACs varied from a minimum of 2 MPs (Anguilla) to a maximum of 25 (Ghana), with an average of 11.6, a value which is nearly identical with what McGee reported.

Furthermore, the analyses revealed that the number of opposition MPs serving on a PAC varied from a minimum of zero MPs (Singapore) to a maximum of 12 (Ghana), with an average of nearly 4.8 opposition MPs serving on a PAC. Dividing the number of opposition MP serving on the PAC by the total number of MPs serving on the committee gives the proportion of opposition MPs serving on the committee. It was found that the proportion varied from a minimum of zero in Singapore to a maximum of 100 percent in Grenada, with an average of 42.3 percent. It was also reported that, with the exception of Anguilla (where the membership on the committee is evenly split between government and opposition)

9. The 24 national PACs had the following regional distribution: ten PACs were African, seven were Caribbean, three were Asian and one each were from Canada, Ireland, South East Asia (Singapore) and New Zealand. The geographic distribution of the 28 sub-national PACs was considerably different: one was from Africa (NW province, in South Africa), eight were from Canadian provinces, four were from the British Isles, eight were from Australia, one was from the Sindh province in Pakistan and the remaining six were from Indian provinces.

and Grenada (where all members of the PAC are selected from the opposition), opposition MPs are greatly outnumbered by MPs affiliated with the government party/coalition; this problem seemed to be particularly acute in Africa.

With regard to the size of the staff, the data showed that the number of staff members at the disposal of a PAC varies from a minimum of zero recorded in the Caribbean (Jamaica, Guyana, Grenada) to a maximum of 20 registered in South Asia (India), with an average of 4.5.

Regarding the political affiliation of the Chair, the survey represented a major departure from what McGee (2002) had indicated. It showed that, in 20 of the 24 countries (or 83.3 percent), the PACs were chaired by an opposition MP, up substantially from the 67 percent reported by McGee.

The survey data were also employed to perform more complex statistical analyses that both supported and contrasted the conclusions drawn in previous studies. Specifically, they showed that some aspects of PAC performance are affected by some PAC characteristics but not by others. No matter how measured, the performance of a PAC is not affected by the size of the PAC or by whether it is chaired by an opposition MP. In contrast, the performance (when measured as the capacity to produce reports) is greatly affected by the size of the staff at the disposal of the committee, while performance (in terms of number of meetings held) is greatly affected by the strength of the opposition parties on the committee.

THE 'NEW STORY'

In this section, we present the data concerning the structure of PACs that were collected in 2009 by WBI. This survey differs from the previous surveys in three basic respects:

1. The number of countries covered is smaller than the number of countries that were surveyed by CPA in 1999, but considerably

THE STRUCTURE OF PUBLIC ACCOUNTS COMMITTEES

larger than the number of countries that were surveyed by WBI in the same year.
2. They differed from one another not only in terms of the number of countries covered in the analysis, but also in terms of compositions.
3. They asked different questions.

With regard to the size of the sample, while the CPA collected data from 70 national and sub-national legislatures for use by McGee and the 2002 WBI-conducted survey gathered data from 52 national and sub-national legislatures, the new (2009) survey gathered data from 58 national and sub-national legislatures (see Table 3.1).

With regard to the composition of the sample, the CPA survey received its 70 responses from countries located in eight different geographic regions (see Table 3.2): there were 18 responses from Africa, 17 from Asia, eight from Australia, six from the British Isles and the Mediterranean, 10 from Canada, six from the Caribbean, Atlantic and the Americas, one from the Pacific, and two from South East Asia, with one anonymous. By contrast, the analyses conducted by Pelizzo (2011) were performed using the data from a 24-country sample that was created by removing the 28 sub-national legislatures from the total number of legislatures that responded to the 2002 WBI survey. Of these, 10 were African, seven were Caribbean, three were Asian, and one each was from Canada, Ireland, South East Asia (Singapore), and New Zealand.

Table 3.1: Size of the sample

	CPA (1999)	WBI 2002	WBI 2009
Number of national and sub-national legislatures	70	52	58
	(used by McGee, 2002)	(used by Pelizzo, 2011; Pelizzo and Stapenhurst, 2007; Pelizzo et al., 2006)	(used here)

The 2009 survey covered 58 national and sub-national legislatures from seven regions. There were four responses from Africa, nine from Asia, 14 from Canada, two from the Caribbean, eight from Europe, eight from the Pacific Region, nine from Asia, and three non-Commonwealth PACs – Indonesia, Thailand and Kosovo.

In spite of the fact that all three surveys sought to gather information on the structural characteristics of PACs, the questionnaire employed in each used somewhat differently worded questions. Thus, it is not possible to precisely compare the level of success that PACs enjoyed over time (as indicated by the committee's ability to achieve certain results); however, the questions were broadly similar and so comparison of results is justified. McGee (2002) asked about the size of the PAC, the proportion of opposition MPs serving on the committee, about the selection of the Chairperson and whether he/she belonged to the government or the opposition. The 2002 and 2009 WBI surveys asked respondents to indicate the political affiliation of the PAC Chair, the number of government and opposition MP serving on committee, and the total size of the committee.

Size of the PAC

With regard to the size of the PAC (see Table 3.3), both McGee (2002) and Pelizzo (2011) found that the average number of MPs serving on the committee was of about 11 MPs — about 11 for McGee and 11.6 for Pelizzo. The 2009 survey presents a very similar picture: the size of a PAC varies from a minimum of 3 MPs to a maximum of 31 MPs, with an average of 10.6.

McGee (2002) also noted that Asian PACs, on average, were larger than elsewhere, because they had on average 17 members, while the average for the other regions was 9 and the average for the Caribbean region was 6. Both WBI surveys give results that are pretty much in line with this. Asian PAC are on average larger than the PACs operating in other countries, the average size being 16.3 MPs in the earlier survey and 18.7 MPs in the later survey. By removing the Asian PACs from the sample, the average size of all other PACs is of about 9 MPs according to McGee, and 9.2 MPs in the 2009 survey. Specifically, we found that the average size of a PAC is 11.3 MPs in West Africa, 10.4 in Europe, 9.4 in Canada, 8.6 in new PACs, 7.7 in Australia and New Zealand, and 7.1 in the Pacific Region.

Table 3.2: Geographic composition of the sample

	CPA (1999)	WBI 2002	WBI 2009
Africa	18	11	4
Asia	17	11	9
Australia and New Zealand	8	9	10
British Isles	6	4	8
Canada	10	9	14
Caribbean	6	7	2
Pacific	1	0	8
South East Asia	2	1	0
Unknown	2	0	0
New			3
Total	70	52	58

While the results from all three surveys are generally consistent, the 2009 data reveals two differences from what McGee had reported. First, they indicate that the smallest PACs are located in the Pacific Region and not in the Caribbean and, second, that the average size of a Caribbean PAC is nearly twice as large as McGee found.[10]

Political Composition

With regard to the presence of opposition MPs on PACs, McGee noted that representation in the PAC generally reflects the balance of political power in the legislature, and that PACs are not dominated by government parties (except for one African legislature, where all the MPs are from the government).

10. We believe that this difference should be attributed to the fact that while McGee covered 6 Caribbean legislatures and 2 Pacific PACs, the 2009 survey was administered only to 2 Caribbean PACs and 8 PACs from the Pacific.

Table 3.3: Size of the PAC

	McGee (2002)	Pelizzo (2011)	Average size of a PAC (2009)
Africa		12.9	11.3
Asia	17	16.3	18.7
Australia and New Zealand		12	7.7
British islands		12	10.4
Canada		17	9.4
Caribbean	6	7.6	14
New	–	–	8.6
Pacific			7.1
South East Asia		8	
Total	11	11.6	10.6

Note: The blanks indicate that the information was either not collected or not made available and the response for the region must be regarded as system missing.

The 2009 survey revealed that the percentage of opposition MPs in PACs varied from a minimum of zero percent in the Cross Rivers legislature (Nigeria) to a maximum of 66.6 percent in Tasmania (Australia), with an average of 37 percent. This means that, while one third of the members serving on a PAC belong to the opposition, the remaining two thirds belong to the government party. This value is nearly 5.3 percentage points lower than was reported by Pelizzo (2011) using the 2002 data. This suggests that many PACs are dominated by the government, which may reduce potential effectiveness.

More importantly, it should be noted that there is considerable variation in how adequately opposition forces are represented across the various regions. Analysis reveals that the percentage of opposition MPs sitting on a PAC is 7.2 percent in West Africa, 17.5 percent in Asia, 37.1 percent in Europe, 37.4 percent in Canada, 38.7 percent in the Pacific, 41.3 percent in the New PACs, 44.2 percent in the Caribbean region, and 50.5 percent in Australia and New Zealand. This would indicate that dominance by the governing party is a particular problem in West Africa and Asia, and we would expect that these PACs would be more effective if they were more balanced in terms of their political representation.

In the 2012 CPA-WBI Study Group held in Victoria (British Columbia, Canada), several participants underlined the importance of members. Some participants underlined that excessive political fragmentation may be detrimental to the proper functioning of PACs (see Box 3.1), while others noted that the success of PACs depends almost entirely on the quality of their members, which is why members sitting on PACs need to receive proper training (see Box 3.2).

Box 3.1: Political fragmentation may undermine performance

The evidence gathered in the course of the Study group revealed that, in India, the fragmentation (of the parliamentary party system) undermines the performance of the PAC. According to one of the participants:

> 'What happens is that there are coalitions now. For the last three or four terms we are having coalitions. In coalitions sometimes the coalition partners have their own vision, own interests, so depending upon that ... that is reflected not only in the parliament but also in the PACs, in the committees. If they are I full agreement with the government, they remain in full agreement with the government, even in the PAC. But if they have different approaches in parliament, then the same difference of approach is reflected in the PAC also. So the Chairman is always in a dilemma on how to create unanimity, because according to our rules, the PAC report has to be unanimous ... That is a tough job under a coalition.'

The analyses that we performed with the data at our disposal confirm the conclusions formulated in the course of the Study Group. The fragmentation of the Indian party system has steadily increased over the years, while the number of reports has significantly declined.

▶

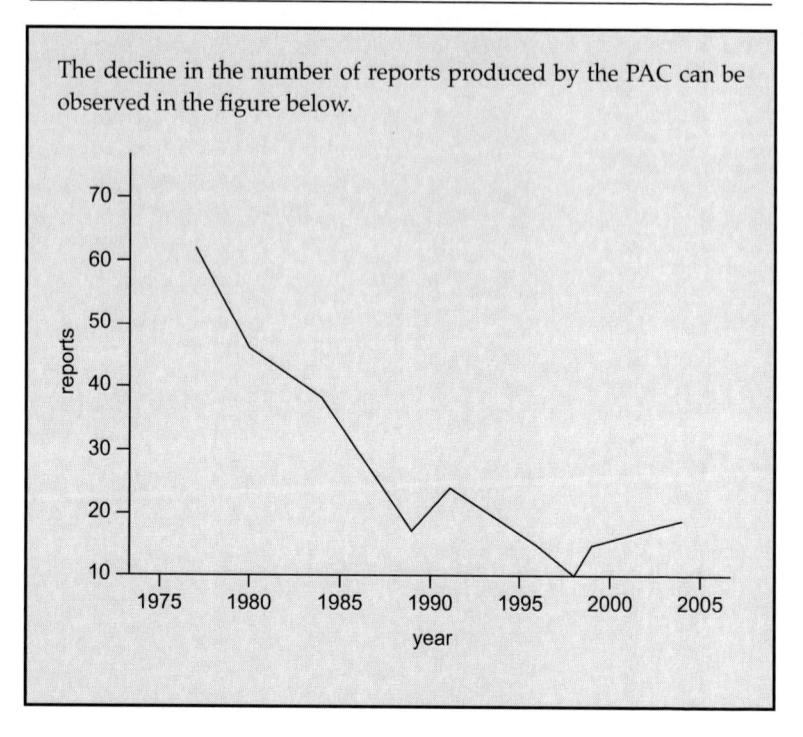

The decline in the number of reports produced by the PAC can be observed in the figure below.

[Figure: Line graph showing reports (y-axis, 10–70) vs year (x-axis, 1975–2005). Reports decline from around 62 in the late 1970s to under 20 by the mid-1990s, with a small rebound thereafter.]

Political Affiliation of the Chairperson

The evidence produced by the 2009 survey is less consistent with the values reported by Pelizzo (2011) than by McGee (2002). The analysis of the 2009 reveals that the PAC Chair is selected from among the opposition members in 70 percent of the cases – close to the 67 percent reported by McGee.[11]

CONCLUSIONS

This chapter discusses the structural characteristics of a Public Accounts Committee, which is important for two reasons: first,

---

11. The reader may recall that Pelizzo (2011) reported that PACs were chaired by 83.3 percent of the 24 countries included in his sample.

THE STRUCTURE OF PUBLIC ACCOUNTS COMMITTEES

> **Box 3.2: The quality of members: evidence from the Study Group**
>
> For Malaysia, quality of members is the solution. If there are good MPs, a lot of problems can be solved.
>
> For Bhutan since we cannot attract the best parliamentarians, how we can make them the best? 'We need a strong secretariat. Once they become a PAC member, then we need to provide orientation and mentoring. Through all these schemes, we need to make them efficient.'
>
> For Liberia, the most pressing needs are proper secretariat 'and to provide training for members on our committee too'.
>
> For Tanzania, training is the solution for many of the problems confronting PACs. 'Training, training, training. All Members of Parliament, whether they come from the developed world or underdeveloped, need training. One piece of training you need to tell Members of Parliament who come to the Public Accounts Committee is that public money has no party ... The people who should be most annoyed for money not being utilized properly are the people in power. If you are a Member of Parliament in power, you should be the first person to frown at or rebuke any public officer who misuses money, because he's not carrying out the promises that were made out to the people.'

PACs have generally been neglected by legislative studies and we believe that no overview of what they are, what their power and the legal authority is, or what they are able to accomplish would be complete if it did not discuss their structural or organisational features. Second, several studies since McGee (2002) have attempted to link PACs' performance to their structural and organisational characteristics.

Specifically, McGee (2002) argued that PAC performance can be influenced by a variety of factors – range of formal powers, working practices, and so on – and that structural (or organisational) characteristics are among the most important of these. He claimed that the success of a PAC can be influenced by the size of the PAC,[12] that, regardless of size, the successful performance of a PAC can be affected by the distribution of power within the committee (that is, how well opposition parties are represented on the committee) and by whether the committee is chaired by a member of the opposition.

These claims have guided practitioners, scholars, and the international community. Some of these claims, such as those on the structure of PACs, have been nearly unanimously supported by more-recent research (Stapenhurst et al., 2005; Pelizzo et al., 2006; Pelizzo and Stapenhurst, 2007; Pelizzo, 2011). However, the validity of others, such as those identifying in the size of the PAC or the political affiliation of the Chair as main determinants of PAC performance have been challenged (Pelizzo, 2011). What matters is not how big a PAC is, but how willing it is to perform its oversight task – a will that cannot be simply explained on the basis of structural and organisational features (Pelizzo and Stapenhurst, 2012). In addition to questions of structure, we also need to consider PAC activity. Chapter 4 further examines the issue of PAC activity.

BIBLIOGRAPHY

McGee, D. 2002. *The Overseers: Public Accounts Committees and Public Spending*, Commonwealth Parliamentary Association and Pluto Press, London.

Pelizzo, R. 2011. 'The Activity of Public Accounts Committees in the Commonwealth: Causes and Consequences', *Commonwealth and Comparative Politics*, vol. 49, no. 4, pp. 528–46.

Pelizzo, R. and Stapenhurst, F. 2007. 'Public Accounts in Comparative Perspective', in Shah, A. (ed.), *Performance Accountability and Combating Corruption*, pp. 379–93, World Bank Institute, Washington DC.

12. Small PACs, he suggested, do not work well, and larger PACs may not work well if they are not adequately resourced.

Pelizzo, R. and Stapenhurst, F. 2012. *Parliamentary Oversight Tools: A Comparative Analysis*. Routledge, London; New York.

Pelizzo, R., Stapenhurst, F., Saghal, V. and Woodley, W. 2006. 'What Makes Public Accounts Committees Work? A Comparative Analysis', *Politics and Policy*, vol. 34, no. 4, pp. 774–93.

Stapenhurst, F., Saghal, V., Woodley, W. and Pelizzo, R. 2005. 'Scrutinizing Public Expenditures. Assessing Performance of Public Accounts Committees', World Bank Policy Research Working Paper 361, World Bank Institute, Washington DC.

4
The Activities of PACs

Chapter 3 notes that the success of Public Accounts Committees (PACs) cannot simply be attributed to their structure. Issues of PAC activity also need to be considered, and, as such, this chapter investigates PAC activity. We not only pay attention to the amount and type of activities (meetings, hearings, inquiries, and reports) that they perform, but we also show that PACs that are more active in one respect are also more active in other respects, that some PACs are more active than others, and that the activism of PACs varies considerably across regions.

THE 'OLD STORY'

The 2002 WBI survey asked PAC chairs to indicate how important they regarded some structural or organisational characteristics for the success of PACs, to indicate how important they regarded certain practices to be, to indicate the frequency with which certain policy relevant results were achieved and, to provide an indication of the amount of activities performed by the PAC. The survey questionnaire (Stapenhurst et al., 2005), asked PAC committee Chairs to indicate the number of meetings held by the PAC, the number of subjects dealt with, and the number of reports issued.[13] This growing interest in PAC activity represents

---

13. The survey questionnaire asked information on the number of meetings, subjects dealt with and reports in question 6. Respondents were given the

an effort to balance earlier work, which tended to focus primarily on PAC structure.

The evidence generated by the survey was used in four studies. The first two studies produced with the data (Stapenhurst et al., 2005; Pelizzo et al., 2006) analysed the importance of organisational features, the importance of committee practices, and the frequency with which certain results were achieved, but they paid no attention to the amount of activities performed. In addition, two more-recent studies (Pelizzo, 2011; Pelizzo and Stapenhurst, 2012) discussed the organisational characteristics of PACs and their ability to achieve certain outcomes, and also analysed the amount of activities performed by the PACs across the Commonwealth and in Africa. The amount of activity performed by the PAC was measured on the basis of the number of meetings and reports in one study (Pelizzo, 2011), and on the basis of the number of meetings, subjects covered, and reports produced in the other (Pelizzo and Stapenhurst, 2012).

The data from the Commonwealth covered 24 countries, 22 of which provided usable answers with regard to the number of meetings that they held. Half of the respondents (11 out of 22) reported that they had held more than 50 meetings in the previous three years, three respondents (13.6 per cent) reported holding between 25 and 49 meetings, two respondents (9.1 percent) reported holding between 10 and 24 meetings, and six respondents (27.3 percent) reported holding between 0 and 9 meetings. With regard to the number of reports, the respondents provided 21 valid responses. Of these, 13 (61.9 percent) indicated that the PAC had issued between 0 and 9 reports, three (14.3 percent) indicated that the PAC had issued between 10 and 24 reports, one (4.8 percent) reported issuing between 25 and 49 reports, and four (19 percent) reported issuing more than 50 reports. If we use the data on the

---

option of choosing one of four options, indicating respectively that the PAC had held between 0 and 9, between 10 and 24, between 25 and 49 or above 50 meetings in the course of the previous three years. Respondents were also asked to indicate in a similar fashion the number of subjects covered by the PAC and the number of reports issued.

number of meetings and reports presented by Pelizzo (2011), we find that the number of meetings and the number of reports are strongly, positively, and significantly related to one another.[14] The analysis of the African data (Pelizzo and Stapenhurst, 2012) generated similar results both in terms of the amount of activities performed and in terms of the correlation between the various types of PAC activity.[15] This would lead to the conclusion that more meetings lead to more reports.

THE 'NEW STORY'

The more recent data collected by the Commonwealth Parliamentary Association (CPA) and the World Bank Institute (WBI) enable us to replicate the analyses conducted in the past and to perform additional ones. With regard to measuring the activities performed by the PAC, the new survey questionnaire introduces some changes over the previous one. First, the amount of activities performed by the PAC is not measured simply on the basis of the number of meetings and reports, but also on the number of inquiries completed and the number of hearings held in the PAC. Second, the new survey questionnaire no longer asks respondents to say whether the amount of activities performed by their PAC falls into one of the above mentioned categories, but rather asks respondents to provide a more precise indication of the exact number of meetings, hearings, inquiries, and reports.

With regard to the number of meetings held by the PAC in the three years prior to the administration of the survey, the more-recent data indicate that this varied from a minimum of 1 meeting (Vanuatu) to a maximum of 248 meetings in Fiji.[16] Globally, PACs held an average of about 46 meetings in a three-year period (or 15.3

14. The correlation analysis yields a Pearson $r = .537$ (sig. =. 012).
15. The correlation analysis yields a Pearson $r = .604$ (sig. = .012).
16. The number of meetings held in Fiji is fairly consistent with what Pelizzo (2010) reported. The data presented by Pelizzo (2010) showed, in fact, that the PAC of the Parliament of Fiji had held 87 meetings in 2006, 41 in 2007, and daily meetings in 2008.

meetings a year), with a standard deviation of 50.4.[17] However, there is considerable variation across regions. The average number of meetings ranges from a minimum of 7.5 meetings held in Africa to a maximum of 94.6 recorded in the Pacific. The reason why the PACs in the Pacific Region have held on average more meetings than the PACs from all the other parts of the world is that the PAC from Fiji reported holding so many meetings. If Fiji is treated as an outlier, and we omit it from the analysis, the rest of the Pacific Region PACs held on average 56.3 meetings in the three years prior to the survey (18.8 per year), which was slightly lower than the British Isles but significantly higher than the average. Additional details can be found in Table 4.1. The data presented in Table 4.1 also suggest that, in the three-year span, the average number of meetings held in South East Asia was 100 meetings (33.3 per year), which would make it the highest regional average in the sample. The only problem with this regional average is that it reflects the number of meetings held in a single country (Thailand) and further data need to be collected to get a more accurate insight into PAC activity in the South East Asian region.

The number of hearings ranges from a minimum of zero (Alberta, Manitoba, Nunavut, Ontario, Queensland and Saskatchewan) to a maximum of 135 (Canada), with an average of 21.8 and a standard deviation of 32.8.[18] There is considerable variation in the number of hearings held across regions, from a minimum of 4 hearings in Africa to a maximum of 55.6 hearings in the Pacific. See Table 4.2 for further details.

There is also a great variation in the number of reports issued across the regions.[19] The number of reports varies from zero

---

17. While the survey was administered to 58 legislatures, responses on the number of meetings were provided only by 48 PACs, while the remaining 10 provided no indication of how often they had met in previous years.
18. The number of valid responses to this question is considerably lower than the number of valid responses for the question concerning the number of meetings. In fact, while 48 respondents out of 58 provided some evidence with regard to the number of meetings, only 36 provided some evidence with regard to the number of meetings that they held.
19. Only 30 of the 58 PACs provided some evidence in this respect.

(Barbados) to 191 (United Kingdom), with an average of 16.5 and a standard deviation of 36.8. The average number of reports varies from a minimum of 2 in Africa to a maximum of 48.2 in the British Isles (see Table 4.3).

Table 4.1: Average number of meetings

Region	Average number of meetings held in a three-year span	Average number of meetings held in a single year
Africa	7.5	2.5
Asia	54	18
Australia and New Zealand	21.6	7.2
British Isles	63.3	21.1
Canada	48.1	16.0
Caribbean[20]	29.5	9.8
Pacific	56.3	18.8
South East Asia	100	33.3

Table 4.2: Number of hearings

Region	Average number of hearings held in a three-year span	Average number of hearings held in a single year
Africa	4.0	1.3
Asia	29.7	8.9
Australia and New Zealand	11.9	3.9
British Isles	36.5	12.2
Canada	28.9	9.6
Caribbean[21]	0	0
Pacific	55.6	18.5
South East Asia	–	–

The number of inquiries varies from a minimum of 1 (Kosovo and Kaduna) to a maximum of 68 (Papua New Guinea), with an average and a standard deviation of 16.9 and 21.7, respectively.

20. This regional average hides the fact that there is considerable variation in the region. The PAC from Barbados held 6 meetings, while the PAC from Jamaica held 53.
21. Note that this value refers exclusively to the number of hearings held in Barbados because Jamaica did not provide any evidence in this regard, nor did it provide evidence with regard to the number of reports produced by the PAC.

THE ACTIVITIES OF PACS

Given the low response rate for this question – only 12 valid responses were provided by the 58 PAC involved in the data collection exercise – it is only possible to compute regional averages for Africa, South East Asia, and the Pacific. Again, there is considerable variation across regions: South East Asian PACs performed on average 4.5 inquiries, African PACs performed an average of 5 inquiries, and the Pacific PACs an average of 30 inquiries over the period of study.[22]

Table 4.3: Number of reports

Region	Average number of reports issued in a three-year span	Average number of reports issued in a single year
Africa	2.0	0.7
Asia	2.3	0.8
British isles	48.2	16.1
Canada	11.6	3.9
Caribbean[23]	53	17.6
Pacific	26.0	8.7
South East Asia	2.5	0.8

Discussion

The data presented in the previous section are interesting for several reasons. It provides information on areas of PAC activity, such as hearings and inquiries, to which previous studies have paid little attention. Prior comparative global analyses of PACs did not provide any information on PAC activity (McGee, 2002; Stapenhurst et al., 2005; Pelizzo et al., 2006), or simply provided some information on the number of meetings and reports (Pelizzo, 2011). Regional studies did provide more information on PAC activity, but they did so only for a fairly small number of countries. However, by presenting information on four different types of

22. Specifically, 8 inquiries were conducted in Fiji, 68 in PNG, 25 in Samoa, and 19 in the Solomon Islands.
23. Note that this value refers exclusively to the number of reports that the Jamaican PAC produced in a three-year span. Since Barbados and the other Caribbean islands did not provide any response in this respect, we were not able to estimate proper regional averages.

PAC activity for a large number of countries, this study provides a more-comprehensive and detailed account of what PACs do.

While further work is required to explore the relationship between PAC activity and output, this data does provide evidence that there is some link between PAC activity and PAC output. However, the broader question of the relationship between PAC activity and PAC performance remains complex and has been assumed but not clearly addressed in much of the earlier work. Exceptions to this – studies that have attempted to link activity and performance – include Pelizzo's (2010) study of seven PACs from the Pacific Region. He measured the activity of the PACs in the region on the basis of the number of meetings held by the committee, number of hearings, number of inquiries completed, and number of reports issued. While this study showed that some Pacific PACs are bigger, better resourced, and more active than others, it showed that there is no detectable relation between these structural factors and the various measures of performance. Pelizzo (2010, p. 127) observed that 'the amount of activities performed by a PAC in one respect tells us very little as to how much that PAC did in another respect. In other words, there seems to be very little correlation between our various indicators of committee activity.'

While a recent study of the organisation, activities, and the overall performance of PACs in the Commonwealth (Pelizzo, 2011) did not directly test whether there is any relationship between the number of meetings and the number of reports produced by a PAC, the analysis of the raw data presented in that study points to a strong, positive, and statistically significant correlation between the two indicators of PAC activity. A similar conclusion was reached by a more recent study of African PACs (Pelizzo and Stapenhurst, 2012), which also found that the number of meetings held by a PAC is strongly, positively, and significantly related to the number of reports it produces.

However, this evidence is far from conclusive. The study of PACs in the Pacific used continuous variables, but the analysis was based on a very small sample. The study on the Commonwealth analysed the data from a much larger sample, but employed categorical variables instead of using the more appropriate continuous one, and the study on African PACs had a small sample and employed categorical data.

Hence, because the results of these studies was inconclusive, we test whether and to what extent the various type of PAC activities are related to one another by using a larger sample and proper continuous variables, and we perform some correlation analyses. The results are presented in Table 4.4. They show that PACs that are more active in one respect are also more active in other respects. In other words, if a PAC produces more reports, for example, it also completes more inquiries, holds more meetings, and conducts more hearings. Alternatively, a PAC that produces fewer reports in all likelihood is one that does not hold many meetings, does not conduct too many hearings, and completes few inquiries, while a PAC that conducts more hearings holds more meetings, completes more inquiries, and produces more reports.

Table 4.4: Correlation analysis (sig.)

	Number of hearings	Number of inquiries completed	Number of reports issued
Number of meetings	.860 (.000)	.043 (.913)	.519 (.006)
Number of hearings	–	.764 (.077)	.803 (.000)
Number of inquiries completed	.764 (.077)	–	.986 (.000)
Number of reports issued	.803 (.000)	.986 (.000)	–

In short, the number of reports is strongly related to all the other measures of activity, the number of hearings is also strongly related to all the other measures of activity, whereas both the number of meetings and the number of inquiries are related to the other measures of activity but not to one another. However, knowing that PACs are more or less active and that higher levels of activity in one respect are associated to higher levels of activity in another respect does not provide any indication as to whether PAC activity is any way related to the promotion of good governance or to other policy-relevant results.

In this respect, when we correlate the number of meetings or the number of hearings held by PACs with the index of state fragility measured by the Brookings Institute, with capacity for controlling corruption (as measured by the World Bank's Governance indicators) and with the gross national income (GNI) per capita (as measured by World Bank's development indicators), we do not find any statistically or substantively significant relationship. In other words, the fact that more meetings or hearings are held does not lead to higher GNI per capita, greater ability to curb corruption, and it is not indicative of greater state capacity. Similarly, higher levels of socio-economic development, a greater state capacity, and a greater ability to control corruption do not lead to more PAC meetings and hearings. The result simply on the basis of activity is very unclear.

What does became clear is that, when we look at the relationship between number of reports produced by a PAC with the indicators on control of corruption and GNI per capita, we find a strong, positive, and significant relationship.[24] This is shown in Figures 4.1 and 4.2. This suggests that PACs in countries with strong control over corruption produce more reports and that PACs in countries with high GNI per capita produce more reports. In effect, a strong and active PAC is strongly linked to control of corruption and economic prosperity. However, the argument could also be reversed and the case made that countries with better control of corruption can afford highly active PACs. While further work is required to explore this issue, Figure 4.3 suggests that there is a clear relationship between economic development and control of corruption. The evidence presented in the annex to this chapter suggests that there is a causal link between PAC activity in terms of reports, control of corruption, and economic prosperity in terms of GNI per capita.

---

24. The case of Barbados is removed from the analysis because it is a clear outlier.

THE ACTIVITIES OF PACs

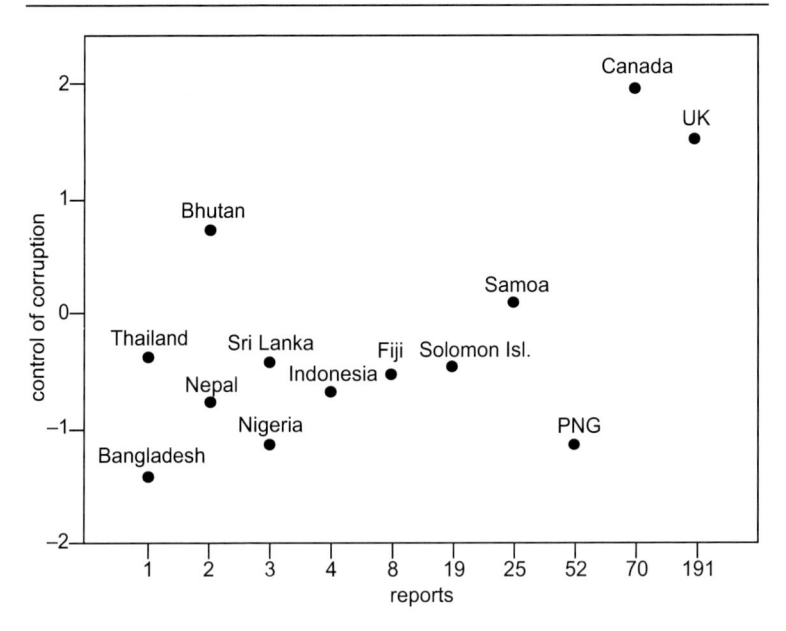

Figure 4.1: Number of PAC reports and ability to control corruption

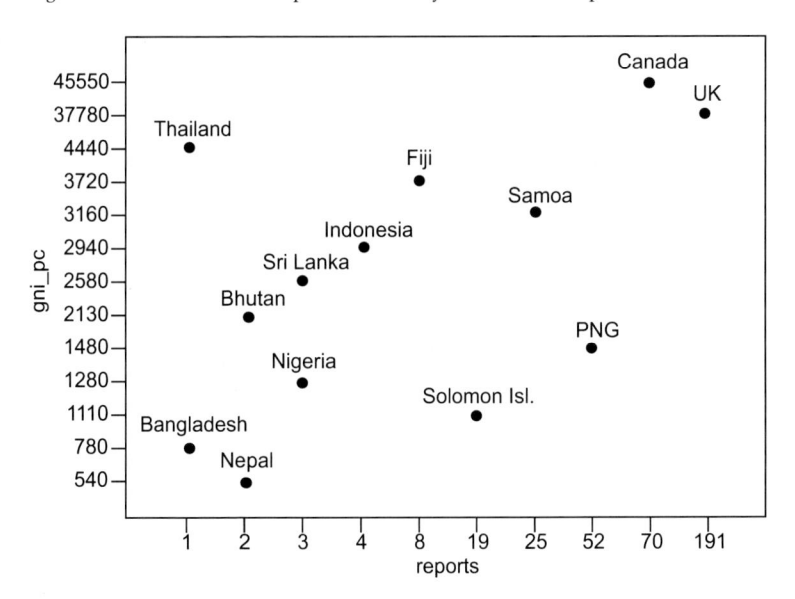

Figure 4.2: Number of PAC reports and GNI per capita

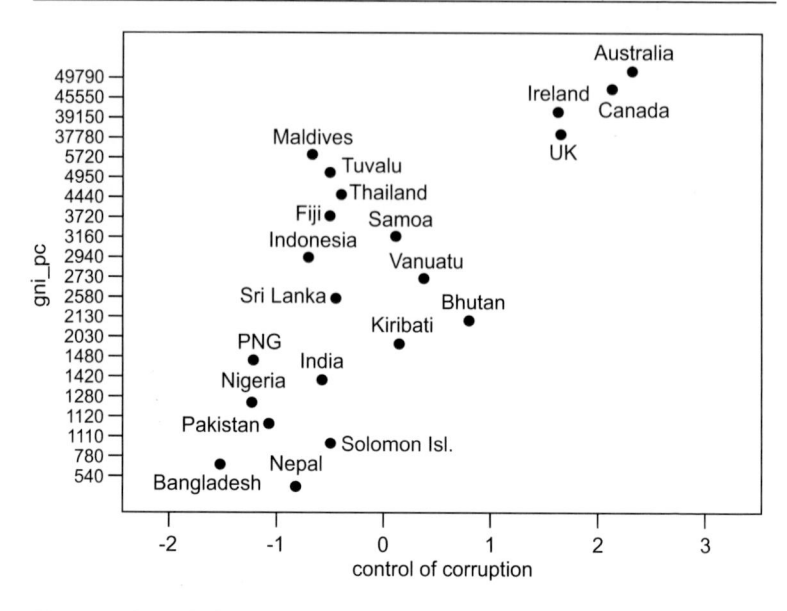

Figure 4.3: Control of corruption and development

CONCLUSIONS

The evidence presented in this chapter is quite informative for two different, albeit related, reasons. The first reason is that the evidence presented here provides a clear indication of what PACs do, of the cross-regional and cross-national variation in the levels of PAC activity, and of the fact that PACs that are more active in one respect tend to be more active also in other respects – though there are of course some exceptions to this generalisation. This evidence represents the most comprehensive assessment of PAC activity worldwide and could be used to evaluate whether, how, and to what extent PAC activity has changed in the course of the past decade. In other words, the first reason why this evidence is relevant is descriptive.

The second reason why the evidence presented here is of some importance is analytical. It shows, in fact, that, while all types of PAC activity tend to go hand in hand, some types of activity are more important than others. This is because some types of PAC activity provide no indication of whether and to what extent a PAC is effective because they have little to no impact in a legislature's ability to keep the government accountable, to be an effective overseer, to contribute to the promotion of good governance, or to curb corruption. In contrast, there are certain types of PAC activity, such as the reports produced by the PAC, that are strongly related to good governance, to the ability to curb corruption, and ultimately to development, which we discuss in a more technical fashion in the annex to this chapter.

But, while technical analyses, regression models, and path analyses will be discussed in greater detail in the annex, the key lesson that emerges from those analyses is very clear. The reason why we find a strong association between PAC performance, good governance, and development is that the effectiveness of PACs in performing their tasks is a major determinant of good governance, transparency, and development. PAC effectiveness is a cause and not a consequence of good governance.

Finally, the evidence presented here teaches an additional lesson; namely, that what makes PACs work effectively in some regions has no impact on PAC performance in other regions, whereas what has no impact on PAC performance in some regions is a major driver of PAC performance in other contexts. This is especially true when considering the size (and the quality) of the staff at the disposal of PACs. Depending on the region, the size of the staff has or does not have an impact on the amount of PAC reports produced by a PAC. The lesson is clear: to increase the effectiveness of a PAC, it is important to understand and address its country-specific needs.

ANNEX – RELATING PAC ACTIVITY, CONTROL OF CORRUPTION AND GNI

In order to assess the impact of PAC activity on a country's level of socioeconomic development, we need to perform more-complex statistical analyses like linear regression and path analysis.

When we perform a linear regression, we try to understand how much change occurs in the dependent variable in response to a unit change in the value of an independent variable by controlling for the effects of another independent variable. We want to understand the relationship between GNI per capita and the number of PAC reports when the ability to control corruption is kept constant. This is done by performing the regression:

$$Y = a + b1X1 + b2X2 + e$$

where Y is the GNI per capita, X1 is the control of corruption variable, X2 is the number of PAC reports, a is the intercept, b1 and b2 are the slopes, and e is the error, we find that the regression model takes the following values:

GNI per capita = 6724.43 + 8807.62 control of corruption + 109.55 number of reports

                (.026)   (.006)   (.047)

This model explains 82.8 percent of the variance of GNI per capita. And, insofar as we regard GNI per capita as a good proxy for socio-economic development, we can conclude that control of corruption and PAC work are two very important determinants of a country's level of socio-economic wellbeing. When we keep the number of PAC reports constant, the GNI per capita increases by more than $8,807 per unit increase in the control of corruption, while the GNI per capita increases by $109.55 per each additional report produced by a PAC. The significance levels reported in the parentheses indicate that each of the regression coefficients is statistically significant.

The problem of regression analysis is that it does not provide a good explanation for *why* PAC activity affects the level of socio-economic development. A more-appropriate way for assessing the causal impact of PAC activity on the level of socio-economic development is represented by path analysis, which we explain in the following paragraphs.

The international community has long held the belief that effective oversight leads to greater control of corruption and that greater control of corruption leads to higher levels of development. In other words the model takes the form shown in Figure 4.4.

```
┌─────────┐  .650   ┌──────────┐  .887   ┌─────────┐
│  PAC    │  ────>  │ Control of│  ────>  │ GNI per │
│ reports │         │corruption │         │ capita  │
└─────────┘         └──────────┘         └─────────┘
```

Figure 4.4: Path analysis r1 = .42 r2 = .78

This path analysis tells us that, when we regress GNI per capita against control of corruption, the model explains 78 percent of the variance of GNI per capita, and that the standardised beta coefficient is .887 and statistically significant (p = .000). While this evidence is consistent with what international organisations have long assumed (namely, that good governance is an important determinant of development), it does not provide an indication of what conditions promote good governance and the ability to control corruption. We run then a second regression. When we regress control of corruption against the number of PAC reports, we find that the model explains 42 percent of the variance, that the number of PAC reports is strongly and positively related to controlling corruption (standardised beta coefficient = .650), and that the relationship is statistically significant (p = .016). By multiplying the two standardised beta coefficients, we find that the indirect effect of PAC reports on GNI per capita is .65*.88 = .57.

It is not difficult to understand why PAC reports are so important for ensuring good governance, curbing corruption, and creating the conditions for socio-economic development. It is through their reports that PACs disclose the findings of their inquiries, pinpoint cases of maladministration, and formulate recommendations on how the expenditure and the management of public resources could be improved.

Given the importance of having an active PAC, what conditions are more conducive to make PACs work effectively and produce more reports?

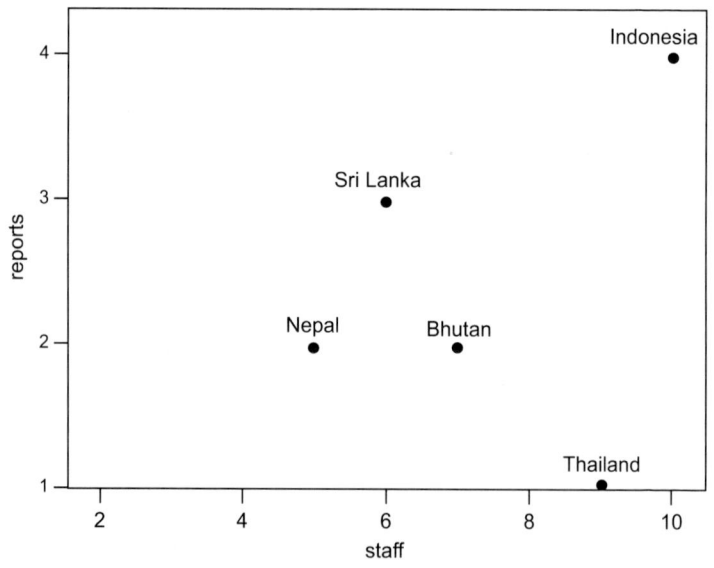

Figure 4.5: Asia

The first answer to this question is that there is not a one-size-fits-all solution. What works in some settings does not work in others. For instance, the size of staff is a strong predictor of PAC performance and number of reports produced in the Pacific (Pelizzo, 2010) and in Eastern and Southern Africa (Pelizzo, 2013), but not elsewhere. In Asia, for example, the relationship between

THE ACTIVITIES OF PACs

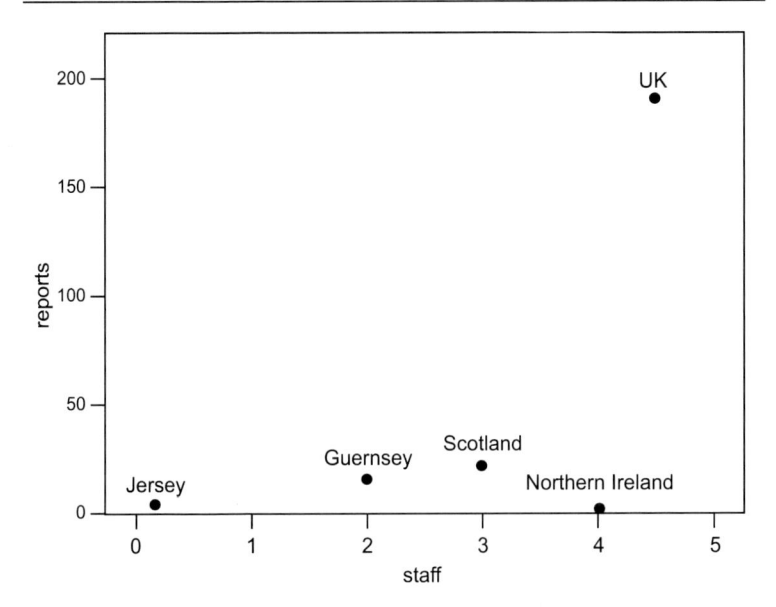

Figure 4.6: British Isles

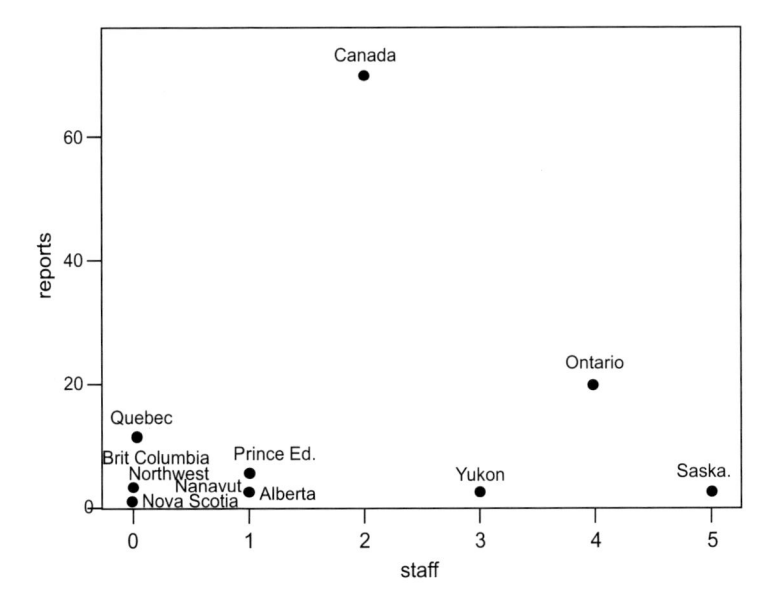

Figure 4.7: Canada

size of PAC staff and number of reports seems to be bell-shaped. In the British Isles, the linearity and the meaningfulness of the relationship is challenged by outliers. In Canada, the production of reports and the size of staff at the disposal of the PAC seem to be independent of one another – see Figures 4.5–4.7. This means that it is necessary to address country-specific needs in order to promote successful and effective PACs.

BIBLIOGRAPHY

McGee, D. 2002. *The Overseers*, London, Verso.
Pelizzo, R. 2010. 'Public Accounts Committees in the Pacific Region', *Politics and Policy*, vol. 38, no. 1, pp. 117–37.
Pelizzo, R. 2011. 'Public Accounts Committees in the Commonwealth: Oversight, Effectiveness, and Governance', *Commonwealth and Comparative Politics*, vol. 49, no. 4, pp. 528–46.
Pelizzo, R. 2013. 'Public Accounts Committees in Eastern and Southern Africa' (unpublished manuscript).
Pelizzo, R. and Stapenhurst, F. 2012. 'Public Accounts Committees in Africa' (unpublished manuscript).
Pelizzo, R., Stapenhurst, F., Saghal, V. and Woodley, W. 2006. 'What Makes Public Account Committees Work? A Comparative Analysis', *Politics and Policy*, vol. 34, no. 4, pp. 774–93.
Stapenhurst, F., Sahgal, V., Woodley, W. and Pelizzo, R. 2005. 'Scrutinizing Public Expenditures', Policy Research Working Paper, no. 3613, World Bank Institute, Washington DC.

5
Capacity of PACs

INTRODUCTION

Chapters 3 and 4 consider the structure and activities of Public Accounts Committees (PACs) and conclude that – with certain exceptions, such as party affiliation of the Chair and representation of the opposition party in PAC membership – these factors were not the critical ones in determining PAC success. It has been widely believed that issues of capacity are central to PAC performance. Capacity is reflected in a number of different ways, which includes the powers and right of access under a PAC mandate, and the staffing and financial resourcing of a PAC. The issue of funding and resourcing is also considered to be critical to the effective operation of an Auditor-General (and therefore by extension the operation of a PAC). We turn to these issues in this chapter.

THE 'OLD STORY'

From an operational perspective, McGee (2002) placed a particular emphasis on the need for a PAC to maintain a bipartisan approach. Therefore, either engagement in an examination of the government's estimates, the inclusion of ministers as members, or calling ministers as witnesses was likely to shift the work of a PAC into the area of policy, undermining a bipartisan approach and increasing the probability of minority reports (McGee, 2002). These kinds of recommendations have often been translated into notions of best practice. In contrast to McGee (2002), Yamamoto (2007) provided a very descriptive study of parliamentary oversight practices in different countries. From this, it can be assumed that normal practice is best practice. However, this is not necessarily the case because it is possible that there are a number of alternative models, and that there is an important relationship between the PAC and key elements of the local environment.

Surveys of PACs have found an enormous diversity in their structures, responsibilities, and work practices (McGee, 2002; Wehner, 2003; Stapenhurst et al., 2005; KPMG, 2006). Nonetheless, they all fit into the 'circle of control' (Chubb 1952, p. 6) of parliamentary financial scrutiny, comprising the submission of estimates to Parliament by the executive, the requirement for money to be expended in accordance with appropriations approved by Parliament, the submission of accounts to Parliament to be audited by the Auditor-General, and the Public Accounts Committee's responsibility to examine expenditure (KPMG, 2006, p. 8).

McGee (2002) couched the role of the PAC in terms of democratic accountability in that the PAC is one of the organisational forms in which Parliament ensures the accountability of government. However, McGee (2002, p. 57) suggests that it is the role of considering the Auditor-General's reports, rather than the more general role of 'examining public accounts', which has become the predominant activity of the PAC in modern times. This has become particularly true with the growth of performance or value-for-money reporting by Auditors-General.

The link between the Auditor-General and the PAC is significant. McGee (2002, p. 11) notes that they are intertwined both in practice and in history. The legislative reforms to create the institution of the modern Auditor-General were accompanied by the procedural reforms that led to the creation of the PAC (McGee, 2002, p. 57). Therefore, the capacity and performance of PACs cannot rightly be considered in separation from the capacity and performance of Auditors-General.

Wehner (2003, p. 24) particularly highlighted the ex post assurance role of the PAC in following up the Auditor-General's reports and identifying the appropriate steps to address any shortcomings. Deploying a feed-forward metaphor, Wehner (2003, p. 24) suggests that the recommendations of the committee can then filter into future budgets, creating continuous and virtuous cycles of improvements in public spending. From this perspective, an effective PAC would be one that impacts future budgets and policy, and capacity is an issue of having the capacity to have said effect. However, this question of what is necessary to build and sustain the capacity of the PAC to effectively (and maybe even efficiently) perform its role needs further consideration. Ultimately, the issue of capacity is dependent on how we understand performance.

THE 'NEW STORY'

The scope of the mandate and legislative powers of PACs is seen as being central to their institutional capacity. While it has often been assumed that the powers of different PACs are reasonably similar, our comparative work would suggest that there are some real differences in this area. We found that the mandate relates to two main issues: (1) the access that a PAC had to areas of government and sections of the private sector who use public funds, and (2) the powers that a PAC has to do its work and conduct its investigations. While certain levels of access and certain investigative powers might be regarded as 'normal practice', there was more divergence on both of these issues than might have been expected.

PAC Right of Access

One fundamental question is around which areas of the public and private sector a PAC has access to. We found (see Table 5.1) that most (but not all) PACs have access to all government agencies (both within and outside of the finance portfolio). However, a few only had conditional access, and one did not have access to agencies outside of the finance portfolio.

Table 5.1: PAC right of access (percent)

Power	PACs that enjoy this power unconditionally	PACs that have this power conditionally	PACs that lack this power	Number of valid answers
Government agencies within the finance portfolio	95	5		55
Government agencies outside the finance portfolio	96	2	2	55
Statutory authorities	86	5	9	55
Government-owned corporations	86	5	9	55
Local government authorities	58	7	35	54
Parliament (and its expenditures)	83	7	10	42
Parliamentarians' expenditures (e.g. staff)	72	2	26	42
Government service providers	56	9	35	55
Government-funded non-governmental organisations	42	17	41	54

Access to statutory authorities and to government-owned corporations was more of a problem because 9 percent of PACs did not have access to these entities and 5 percent had conditional access. Unconditional access to local government authorities (58 percent), to government service providers (56 percent), and to government-funded non-governmental organisations (43 percent) was also much lower than might have been expected. When combined with conditional access, this increases to 65 percent for local government providers, 65 percent for government service providers, and 59 percent for government-funded non-governmental organisations. Therefore, while around two-thirds of the PACs have some capacity to 'follow the government dollar', many do not, and a number of those that do have the legislative capacity for this kind of work have conditional limitations on their powers.

In contrast, a surprisingly large number of PACs have the ability to review the spending of both Parliament (83 percent) and Parliamentarians (72 percent). These percentages increased to 90 percent and 74 percent, respectively, when considering which PACs had a conditional or unconditional mandate to do this kind of work. Given the 2009 UK scandal around parliamentary expense claims (the political sensitivity around addressing this kind of issue), it is questionable whether a mandate to review parliamentary and Parliamentarian spending is often exercised.

Therefore, most PACs have a very broad mandate to explore freely within government agencies, and quite a number have the ability to follow spending out of the government and into private organisations that receive government funding. However, when considered on a regional level, clear differences emerge (see Table 5.2).

While it is clear that PACs in Africa tend to have a reduced right of access to government agencies both within and outside of the finance portfolio (only 75 percent have unconditional access as opposed to 100 percent from many other regions), there was some difference between legal right of access and what some jurisdictions could actually access. Politically sensitive issues such as mining leases awarded by the government to private businesses and the details of foreign debts could pose problems.

On a broader level, there are issues around the power of PACs to 'following the public dollar'. Table 5.1 shows that the majority of PACs have unconditional (or conditional) access to most areas of central government (local government is a more variable issue). However, there are real and significant restrictions when it comes to examining the use of public funds by public service providers (35 percent with no access) and even more restrictions for govern-

Table 5.2: Percentage of PACs that have unconditional access

Power	Africa	Asia	Aus/NZ	British Isles	Canada	Caribbean	Pacific	South East Asia
Government agencies within the finance portfolio	75	100	100	100	92	100	100	50[25]
Government agencies outside the finance portfolio	75	100	100	100	92	100	100	100
Statutory authorities	75	100	80	67	92	50	88	100
Government-owned corporations	75	100	80	67	92	100	100	100
Local government authorities	50	75	30	38	39	100	100	100
Parliament (and its expenditures)	75	86	70	100	–	100	75	100
Parliamentarians' expenditures (e.g. staff)	75	86	60	67	–	–	86	50
Government service providers	50	100	50	67	46	0	57	50
Government-funded non-governmental organisations	50	50	20	67	46	50	50	50

25. The Indonesian PAC reported to enjoy this power only on a conditional or restricted basis.

ment-funded non-governmental organisations (41 percent with no access).

The question of PAC access to local government spending shows two completely different approaches, and this is strongly region-specific as Table 5.2 shows. For Australia, New Zealand, Canada, and the British Isles, around one third of the PACs have unconditional access to local government entities. However, half of the African PACs and all of the Caribbean and Pacific Island PACs studied have this same unconditional access. The most logical explanation for this finding is that the smaller jurisdictions in the Pacific and the Caribbean combine these oversight roles, while the larger ones have this separate. However, this does not tell the whole story because some large jurisdictions such as Indonesia combine oversight levels with the Indonesian PAC having a right of access to national, regional, and local government entities.

In reviewing the mandated right of access, we would suggest that most PACs have a broad access to all government agencies both within and outside of the finance portfolio. Those who have constitutional restrictions in this area should seek to have their mandate extended. Many PACs have also obtained the power to 'follow' government money and investigate government and non-government service providers. PACs should also be encouraged to extend their mandate in this area. However, some PACs have oversight for local government activity and others do not. It seems that combined oversight is a particularly effective approach for small jurisdictions.

PAC Powers

In addition to the diversity in mandate scope, there is both diversity and consistency in the roles and powers of PACs. Table 5.3 indicates that, while all PACs have the power to examine accounts and financial affairs (although for a few this power is conditional), the majority of PACs confine their role to the ex post review process with ex ante review of budget estimates resting with other committees or other parts of the parliamentary system. Table 5.4

Table 5.3: PAC powers (percent of PACs)

	Have this power unconditionally	Have this power conditionally	Lack this power	Number of valid answers
Examination of accounts and financial affairs	96	4	0	55
Consideration of budget estimates (other than Audit Office)	22	0	78	54
Efficiency, economy and effectiveness of government policy	80	0	20	49
Efficiency and economy of policy implementation (value for money)	94	0	6	51
Effectiveness of government implementation (delivery of outcomes)	90	0	10	51
Undertake self-initiated inquiries	72	0	28	46
Examine AG Compliance reports	94	0	6	55
Examine AG Performance reports	91	0	9	55
Refer matters to the AG	84	7	9	55

suggests that it is the smaller jurisdictions from the Caribbean and the Pacific and some of the smaller regional jurisdictions from the larger countries that combine the ex ante budget review role with the ex post financial review role.

What is surprising is that, despite McGee's (2002) injunction, many PACs studies (with the clear exception of the Caribbean – Table 5.4) have the power to examine the efficiency and effectiveness of policy rather than just the implementation of that policy. Generally, PACs have quite broad mandates with wide-ranging powers, with some notable difference around the

Table 5.4: Account and operations, regional trends – percentage of respondents

	Africa	Asia	Aus/NZ	Canada	Caribbean	British Isles	Pacific	South East Asia
Examination of accounts and financial affairs	100	100	90	100	100	100	100	50
Consideration of budget estimates (other than Audit Office)	0	28.5	30	7.1	50	25	37.5	0
Efficiency, economy and effectiveness of government policy	100	100	77.7	78.5	0	62.5	57.1	100
Efficiency and economy of policy implementation (value for money)	100	100	100	92.8	50	100	71.4	100
Effectiveness of government implementation (delivery of outcomes)	100	100	90	92.8	50	100	71.4	50
Undertake self-initiated inquiries	50	66.7	80	57.1	100	50	42.8	100
Examine AG Compliance reports	100	100	90	100	100	100	75	100
Examine AG Performance reports	100	100	90	100	100	100	50	100
Refer matters to the AG	75	100	70	78.6	100	100	75	100

consideration of budget estimates, the examination of policy, and the self-initiation of enquiries.

At a regional level, the nature of the mandate differences become more evident. The examination of estimates is more common in the Caribbean and in the Pacific. This would suggest that combining the ex post and ex ante review is also a practical response to smaller jurisdictions. The issue of PAC review of government policy and the power to self-initiate inquiries is not such a clear pattern. The smaller jurisdictions of the Pacific and the Caribbean tend to be more restrictive on the power of PACs to review government policy, while the power to undertake self-initiated inquiries is highly variable across all regions. Perhaps the most surprising point is that a number of Pacific Islands (50 percent) lack the power to review performance audit reports produced by the Auditor-General, and some (25 percent) lack the power to refer matters to the Auditor-General. These are important powers to grant a PAC.

Capacity and Resources

The issue of capacity is not only related to the mandate and scope of work of PACs, but also to the staffing and financial resources available to them. Collecting information on the funding of PACs proved difficult because, for many jurisdictions, no information was provided on funding and, for those that were, it is difficult to compare because of the differences in spending power between different countries. However, the financial resources provided fell into three general categories. Most committees provide some form of allowance for committee members, travel and other committee costs, and costs associated with committee staff. In some countries, staff cost is recorded as a cost of the PAC, while, in others, it is included with the general costs of parliamentary administration.

Because most jurisdictions provide some form of member allowance and travel cost, the noticeable difference in resourcing, and therefore capacity, is best reflected in the number of staff available to a PAC. The diversity in the number of staff available is dramatic: Fiji and the Maldive Islands have no staff, while Nigeria has 19 staff. The mean number of staff across the jurisdictions studied was 3.3. There is a general relationship between the number of staff and the number of members involved in a PAC. In effect, small PACs have just a few staff and large PACs have more staff. But there are outliers and exceptions. The PACs from Bhutan and Indonesia are among the best-staffed PACs in our sample despite the fact that they are much smaller than PACs operating in other jurisdictions (Australia, Canada, the United Kingdom); meanwhile, in some of the largest PACs (Nepal, Sri Lanka), the size of the PAC staff is a fraction of what it is in the small but well-staffed South East Asian PACs (see Figure 5.1).

Case: PAC funding in Papua New Guinea (PNG)

In PNG, the PAC is funded through the main Parliament budget and allocated on a quarterly basis. The amount of funding is based on estimates submitted by the PAC, and the only role that the PAC plays consists in sending estimates to Parliament's accounts division, which distributes funds to the committees. In 2005–06, the expenditures were 1.2 million.

Case: PAC funding Thailand

In Thailand, funding is indicated by annual budget, all committees get Baht 2.3 million, and the PAC plays no role in setting up its own budget. The Thai PAC spent Baht 1.2 million on members allowances, Baht 2.3 million on travels and other allowances, Baht 2.4 million on staff, and Baht 4.2 million on administrative costs.

The general relationship between staff number and membership also holds true at a regional level with the PACs with a relatively small membership in islands and small states having very small staff cohorts (quite often these lack a dedicated staff member). From a practical perspective, it seems to be important that a PAC has at least one dedicated staff member. However, there are some notable outliers. The South East Asian jurisdictions of Indonesia and Thailand have a relatively large number of staff, Nigeria is notably resourced in this area, and a few (such as Fiji, the Maldives and Jersey) have few if any staff.

Staffing is believed to be a very important condition for the successful performance of a PAC. Participants in the Study

FOLLOWING THE MONEY

Group reiterated this point. Staffing is needed especially when the committee is confronted with a heavy workload. The only way of coping with such a workload is having proper support from the staff (see Box 5.3).

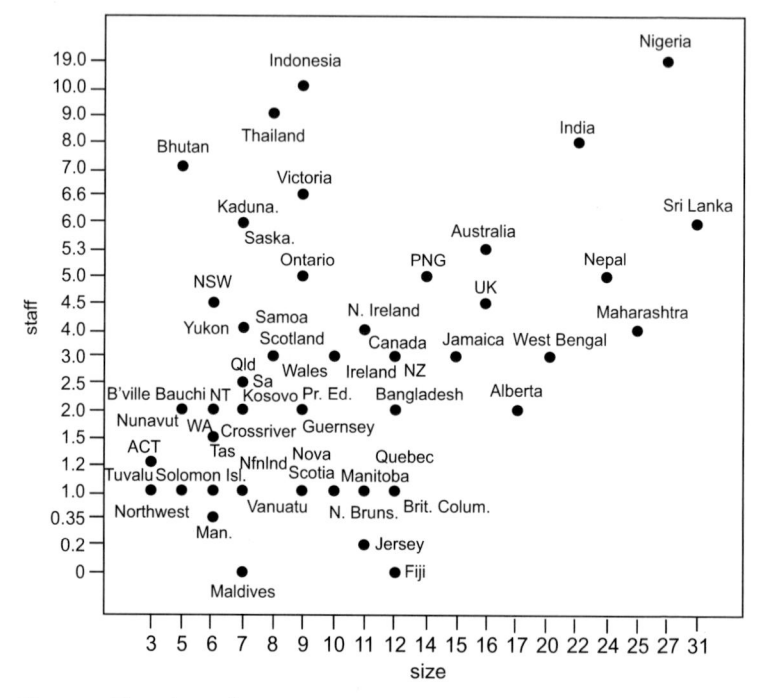

Figure 5.1: The relationship between parliamentary staff and number of members

---

Box 5.3: The importance of the staff: evidence from the Study Group

For Trinidad and Tobago, the output of the PAC is negatively affected [by the fact that they have too few staff members]. It's inversely proportional to the support staff they have. They need more people. If they had more, they would be able to produce reports on a more timely basis and also get information out of the entities on a more timely basis. This one person [of the staff] is certainly overworked.

While it is clear that PACs that do not have adequate staff support may struggle to perform their roles, a larger size does not necessarily lead to superior or exceptional performance. While in some instances a large staff may signal a Parliament's or a political system's commitment to making a PAC function effectively, in other instances the recruitment of a large staff may have an entirely different meaning. For instance, it could signal the political system's commitment to create employment, to distribute material and symbolic benefits, and to reward political support groups in order to increase the legitimacy of the institution and of the ruling elite. This is the reason why, as we report in the previous chapter, a larger staff makes the PAC more effective in some regions but not in others. One point that emerged quite clearly from the Study Group is that the quality of the staff is more important than its size. Study group members argued that there were two key elements relating to the quality of staff. First, the PAC secretariat needs to be effective and experienced. This strongly supports the argument for an experienced and stable secretariat of at least one individual who can support the PAC's function. The second critical element for ensuring the quality of PAC staff is proper training not only for MPs who became PAC members but also and more importantly for PAC support staff. There was some difference in where and how this could be provided. Participants suggested it could be provided by a combination of CPA training, local orientation training for new PAC members and staff, and mentoring from past committee members and staff members. With regard to the knowledge that members may require to perform their committee duties, such as the need to understand public accounts and the performance audit work of an Auditor-General, it was also suggested that members should be equipped with an introduction to public administrative law (and procedure) so that they can understand the legal context and engage with senior departmental officials. It is particularly important that PAC members understand the difference between a biased and fair hearing and how these can be best conducted.

It was also agreed that, once members are selected and trained, they needed a reasonable period in the role to consolidate their experience and to develop independence. In fact, PAC member capacity related to a combination of training, qualifications, and experience. However, while some jurisdictions provided relatively long terms (three to five years) for PAC members, for others this changed much more often (sometimes each session of Parliament). There was a strong view that longer-term commitment to a PAC was critical for capacity and effectiveness.

THE PROBLEM OF PERFORMANCE

If the issue of capacity has posed problems for parliamentary experts, the question of performance seems to be even more of an issue. This is an extension of the issue of output discussed in Chapter 4.

When the number of activities (meetings, hearings, reports, inquiries) is correlated with the score that countries receive in terms of right of access, power and operations, and Auditor-General reports, we find that there is no relationship whatsoever between these powers and the amount of activity performed. When asked whether PACs have mechanisms to measure performance, most PAC indicated that they did not.

PACs that do have some form of reporting function tended to have some form of annual reporting around activity and number of investigations conducted. KPMG's (2006) study of PACs in Australia and New Zealand suggested that that 'one size does not fit all' because there were a variety of structures and institutional practices across the different PACs analysed. However, there was general support for the notions of political neutrality, bipartisanship, consensus, and good governance. They reported that most of the PACs that they studied provided annual reports and website disclosure, which provide details of their activities, members, and sometimes details of government responses to the PAC recommendations (KPMG, 2006). Of the few PACs that provided quantifiable information on performance, the most notable were the Victorian Public Accounts and Estimates

Committee, who reported key performance indicators such as the percentage of recommendations accepted by government, the number of reports completed, and the number of submissions received. A number of other PACs also had explicit performance measures as part of their annual reports such as the Queensland PAC, who reported their publications tabled, hearings, meetings, and inspections as part of the Parliamentary Service annual report, and the NSW PAC, who reported their activities annually along with the number of report recommendations adopted by parliament in their published Annual Review. The Australian Federal PAC (Joint Committee of Public Accounts and Audit – JCPAA) did not publish performance data but had an internal performance review system that focused on reviewing the speed and responsiveness of government's response to the committee recommendations.

Study Group members highlighted many of the conventional performance measures such as an analysis of uptake by the executive from the recommendations of the Auditor-General and the PAC. Study Group members found the notion that action was taken on the basis of PAC recommendations to be very satisfying. There were also comments about process measures such as the numbers and regularity of meetings. In addition, there was the recognition that an effective PAC could contribute to reductions in waste and cost savings. However, this contribution is not always easy to measure.

At a structural level, the PAC could contribute to the quality of the public financial management within the country. First, it was recognised that the relationship between the PAC and the Auditor-General was critical, and the performance of an effective PAC was reflected (at least in part) in an effective Auditor-General. Therefore, a PAC could support the independence, resourcing, and activities of the Auditor-General. This could also extend to recognition among accountable officers that they were eventually going to account to account to someone. 'Yeah, we are doing this, but at the end of the year we are going to meet the PAC.' This need to extend to both a recognition that the public taxpayer is the ultimate client of the PAC and therefore some form of stakeholder (both internal and external) feedback or evaluation could be a valuable form of performance evaluation for PACs.

CONCLUSIONS

The scholarly literature has suggested several ways in which the PAC performance could be measured. While each of the proposed solutions has some merits, which we see in the previous chapter, the drafting and the release of reports represents one of the most compelling way of assessing PAC performance and activity. PACs that produce more reports and formulate more recommendations make a more significant contribution to good governance and to the reduction of corruption and administrative malpractice. The evidence we present in the previous chapter shows that the production of PAC reports can be boosted by the availability of larger cohorts of staff members in some settings, but not in others.

What matters is not so much how many staff members are placed at the disposal of a PAC, but rather how well they are trained to do their job. Training is crucial both for support staff and for MPs serving on the committee. Hence, the key policy recommendation that we can draw from this chapter is that legislature should provide MPs and staff members with more and better training. However, it is recognised that small and developing countries face particular problems, which are discussed in Chapter 6.

BIBLIOGRAPHY

Chubb, B. 1952. *The Control of Public Expenditure*, Oxford University Press, Oxford.

Jacobs, K. and Jones, K. 2009. 'Legitimacy and Parliamentary Oversight in Australia. The Rise and Fall of Two Public Accounts Committees', *Accounting, Auditing and Accountability Journal*, vol. 22, no. 1, pp. 13–34.

Johnston, N. and von Trapp, L. 2008. 'Strengthening Parliament – Strengthening Accountability', *Parliamentary Strengthening Program*. World Bank Institute, Washington DC.

Jones, K. 1987. 'The Origins of the Victorian Parliamentary Public Accounts Committee'. MA, University of Melbourne, Melbourne.

Jones, K. and Jacobs, K. 2006. 'Governing the Government: The Paradoxical Place of Public Accounts Committees', *Australasian Parliamentary Review*, vol. 21, no. 1, pp. 63–79.

Jones, K. and Jacobs, K. 2009. 'Public Accounts Committees, New Public Management and Institutionalism: A Case Study', *Politics & Policy*, vol. 7, no. 5, pp. 1023–46.

KPMG. 2006. *The Parliamentary Public Accounts Committee: an Australian and New Zealand Perspective*. KPMG, Canberra.

Lipsky, M. 1980. *Street-Level Bureaucracy. Dilemmas of the Individual in Public Service*. Russell Sage Foundation, New York.

Martin, J. E. 2004. *The House: New Zealand's House Representatives 1854–2004*, Dunmore Press, Palmerston North.

McGee, D. 2002. *The Overseers: Public Accounts Committees and Public Spending*, Commonwealth Parliamentary Association and Pluto Press, London.

McKinnon, M. 2003. *Treasury: The New Zealand Treasury 1840–2000*, Auckland University Press, Auckland.

Monk, D. 2010. 'A Framework for Evaluating the Performance of Committees in Westminster Parliaments', *Journal of Legislative Studies*, vol. 16, no. 1, pp. 1–13.

Modell, S., Jacobs, K. and Wiesel, F. 2007. 'A Process (Re)turn? Path Dependencies, Institutions and Performance Management in Swedish Central Government', *Management Accounting Research*, vol. 18, no. 4, pp. 453–75.

O'Flynn, J. 2007. 'From New Public Management to Public Value: Paradigmatic Change and Managerial Implications', *Australian Journal of Public Administration*, vol. 66, no. 3, pp. 353–66.

Pelizzo, R., Stapenhurst, R., Saghal, V. and Woodley, W. 2006. 'What Makes Public Accounts Committees Work?', *Politics and Policy*, vol. 34, no. 4, pp. 774–93.

Stapenhurst, R., Johnston, N. and Pelizzo, R. 2006b. *The Role of Parliament in Curbing Corruption*, World Bank Institute, Washington DC.

Stapenhurst, R., Sahgal, V., Woodley, W. and Pelizzo, R. 2005. *Scrutinising Public Expenditure. Assessing the Performance of Public Accounts*

Committees, World Bank Policy Research Working Paper 3613, World Bank Institute, Washington DC.

Uhr, J. 1998. *Deliberative Democracy in Australia. The Changing Place of Parliament*, Cambridge University Press, Cambridge.

Uhr, J. 2001. 'Parliament and Public Deliberation: Evaluating the Performance of Parliament', *UNSW Law Journal*, vol. 24, no. 3, pp. 708–23.

Wehner, J. 2003. 'Principles and Patterns of Financial Scrutiny: Public Accounts Committees in the Commonwealth', *Commonwealth and Comparative Politics*, vol. 41, no. 3, pp. 21–36.

6
Developing Countries and Smaller Parliaments

Both McGee (2002) and our Study Groups (1999 and 2012) recognised that Public Accounts Committees (PACs) in developing countries or in smaller Parliaments (and by implication smaller jurisdictions) face particular challenges. McGee (2002) highlighted four linked issues. First, PACs in small Parliaments and in developing countries can face problems of limited resources to fund their committee or to fund the work of the Auditor-General. This issue of capacity is reflected in the second challenge, which relates to the difficulties in finding members to serve on a PAC and in getting serving members to attend PAC meetings. McGee (2002) also highlighted the lack of legal protection for the Auditor-General's office in some developing countries, which can become a particular issue when an Auditor-General identifies fraud and corruption. At a more general level, there can be challenges (which are not restricted to small and developing jurisdictions) where there is a lack of understanding of the role of the PAC among parliamentary members, the bureaucracy, and the wider public.

McGee (2002, p. 84) suggested solutions to these challenges, which include (a) a rational review of parliamentary funding that takes into account the essential oversight functions performed by the PAC, and (b) assistance and training for members and secretariat of PACs. In addition, it might be possible to draw secretariat assistance from an Auditor-General's office. However, further work is required to explore both the challenges and the proposed solutions.

From a practical perspective, McGee (2002, p. 83) combines the issue of small Parliaments and developing countries. While we recognise that both of these issues may be linked to broader issues of PAC capacity and therefore be related, this relationship is not inevitable. Therefore (if we ignore the question of small Parliaments), can we see a relationship between PAC size and economic development? Figure 6.1 suggests that this is not a simple linear relationship. In Figure 6.1 we correlate the size of the PAC with the level of development (measured on the basis of the gross national income (GNI) per capita, 2011 World Bank Development Indicators). There is not a neat relationship between these variables but there are patterns. Most developed countries have PACs with between 12 and 18 staff members. Many of the smaller (and less-developed) jurisdictions have smaller (sometimes much smaller) PACs. However, a number of the jurisdictions with lower GNI (and by implication less developed) have larger PACs.

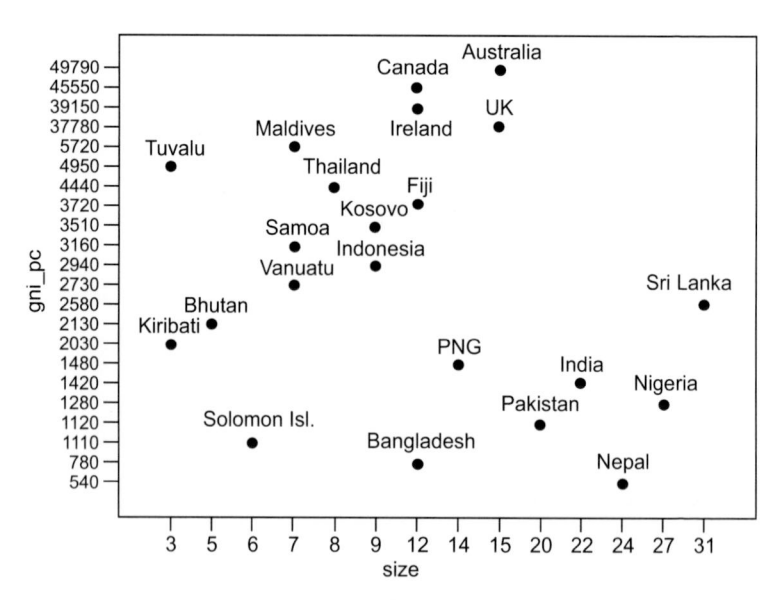

Figure 6.1: PAC size and GNI per capita

This distinction between small and developed jurisdictions can be further explored when McGee's comments on the problems of development jurisdictions are explored from the perspective of state fragility. In other words, where there is weak state capacity and legitimacy, historically weak governance, and high levels of sensitivity to internal and external shocks, PAC members could be expected to have less opportunities to develop the expertise required to perform their role, be less able to rely on bureaucratic and administrative systems, have less access to staff support and potentially face higher levels of corruption and mismanagement. In short, they have a very difficult job. However, is the response to state fragility to have smaller or larger PACs? One might expect to find smaller PACs in small and developing jurisdictions because the number of members which the required expertise might be quite limited. However, larger PACs could be a reasonable response to the workload because they would share the demands of oversight and governance across more people.

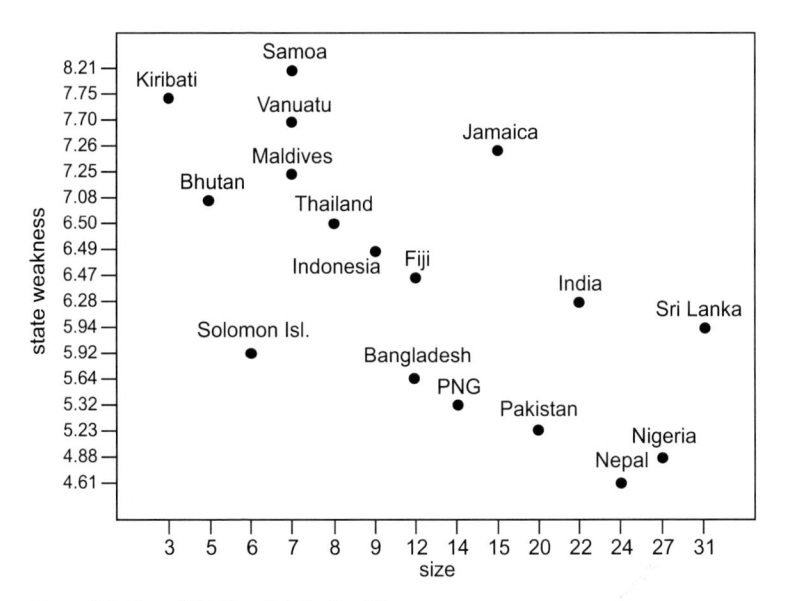

Figure 6.2: Size of PAC and state fragility

The Brookings Institute has developed an Index of State Weakness for the countries of the developing world, introduced in Chapter 4. This index is expressed on a 10-point scale. This index is computed by considering five variables: economic, political, security, social welfare, and GNI per capita. On the basis of how a country fares in each of these dimensions, it is assigned a score. On the basis of the scores that a country has received in each of these dimensions, an overall score from 0 to 10 is computed. This overall score is the index of state weakness: the lower the score, the lower the state capacity and therefore the higher the state fragility; whereas the higher the score, the higher the state capacity and the lower the state fragility. We use this measure to assess capacity and to see whether and to what extent it is related to size. In order to do so, we produced a scatter plot (Figure 6.2) in which we display the data pertaining to the size of the PACs on the x axis, the values of state weakness/capacity on the y axis.

Figure 6.2 suggests that there is a relationship between PAC size and state fragility. Generally, more-fragile states have larger PACs and less-fragile states have smaller PACs. However, this is something of an over-simplification because it is clear that many of the smallest PACs (3–5 members) are in the smallest jurisdictions regardless of state fragility issues. There seems to be a middle-sized group of PACs that have between 8 and 15 members but some of the most fragile states have the largest PACs. Large PACs can be seen as a response to complex and challenging governance and oversight. The question that remains is whether it is an effective or an ineffective response. However complex and challenging, small Parliaments have small PACs because there is really no alternative.

One expected response to issues of state fragility (and the associated challenges of governance and oversight) would be the development of a more extensive number of support staff. Therefore, do we see a clear relationship between state fragility and staff numbers? The answer to this question is no. Some of the weak states had a large number of staff and some did not. In contrast, some more-robust states had many staff and some did not. While access to experienced and capable staff is recognised as a critical success factor, substantial expansion of staff numbers is not necessarily helpful.

Issues and Solutions

From a practical perspective, the issues McGee (2002) highlighted remain a challenge. However, some strategies and approaches exist to solve them. While the issue of resourcing remains a challenge, this can be addressed in conjunction with a wider parliamentary and social awareness of the PAC's work. Because the PAC focuses on issues that are important to the Parliament and to the public, the case for necessary enhanced resourcing becomes stronger. In addition, joint identification by a PAC and an Auditor-General of the aspects of public sector activity and spending that pose particular risks could be a productive way to maximise the benefits of the work of a PAC and an Auditor-General in a setting where resources are constrained. It is the performance audit as opposed to the financial audit work of an Auditor-General that is the driver for PAC investigations and hearings in many of the larger and more-developed jurisdictions. However, performance audits are not always produced in smaller and less-developed jurisdictions. Therefore, opportunities exist to explore internal control weaknesses that have been identified by internal auditors or as part of the broader programme of financial audit where these control weaknesses have serious risk implications for maladministration or misuse of resources. This approach was illustrated by the Isle of Man.

Case: Isle of Man

The Isle of Man is a small, self-governing British Crown Dependence located in the Irish Sea whose Parliament (Tynward) claims to be the oldest continuously ruling body in the world. However, the elected body (House of Keys) is very small with only 24 members and an upper House of 11 members. The PAC has five members and is supported by one Clerk. There approach is that the members of the PAC are also part of the other policy-review committees. They receive and review audit reports from the internal auditors (they lacked an Auditor-General at this stage) and investigate serious issues of maladministration or misuse of resources, but they pass policy issues to the policy-review committees. However, they recognise that, in such a small jurisdiction, there is a danger that senior ministers may be unwilling to engage with the PAC or that PAC members may be unwilling to 'rock the boat' and challenge senior ministers.

The PAC on the Isle of Man illustrates that a small jurisdiction can overcome the small number of members and limited staffing by focusing on the most important work and working closely with (and delegating the more policy-orientated work to) other oversight and review committees.

Realistically, there is a need to work with what is available. While this may lead to contradicting some of the 'ideal PAC' aspects (Stapenhurst et al., 2005), these should be seen as ideals rather than absolutes. One example would be the Solomon Islands where the Auditor-General functions as the secretary of the PAC, or Denmark where the PAC members are external to Parliament. Both of these approaches allow a PAC to access external expertise. This approach is consistent with McGee's (2002) suggestion of looking to the Auditor-General or to local universities for training and support. The Study Group emphasised the critical importance of good training and support for PAC members who do not necessarily have a pre-existing background in governance and financial oversight.

Case: Bhutan

Bhutan has a bicameral system with 30 members, the majority (25) elected as representatives of the districts (and five appointed by the King). The lower House consists of 55 directly elected members. The PAC is a joint committee of both Houses and it has five members. There is a close working relationship, three of the five PAC members have financial backgrounds, and all members of the Bhutan Parliament are required to have a university degree. As a new Parliament, developing the procedures and the expertise of the staff has been a challenge. There is a strong national agenda to reduce corruption (including support from the King). However, the small population and the close-knit society make issues of auditing and corruption sensitive because of potential personal and family relationships.

The financial and accounting expertise of Bhutan PAC members was a clear advantage to the work of the PAC. However, wider education of PAC staff and the public was necessary. Bhutan also highlights the challenges associated with addressing issues of waste and corruption in relatively small close-knit societies.

In the Pacific Region, most countries and most PACs (with the exception of a few such as Papua New Guinea) are small. They normally have four or five members. One of the challenges is that they can easily be dominated by government members, and about half of them are chaired by the government. While both McGee (2002) and PAC best practice (Stapenhurst et al., 2005) would suggest that ministers (or shadow ministers) should not be members of a PAC, that recommendation is not always followed. In addition, a number of Pacific nations have a third parliamentary chamber (containing traditional or noble representatives). In some countries, where this third chamber does not exist, members of the nobility may be directly appointed to the legislative assembly. These kinds of arrangements can pose particular challenges to the oversight and governance role of a PAC, and particular care may be required to design an arrangement that allows both effective oversight and properly respects local conditions.

Case: ACT Assembly Australia

The ACT Assembly is a unicameral territory in Australia. The legislative assembly has 17 directly elected members. For a long time, there were just three members and the committee was chaired by a minority member. This changed in 2012, and now all committees have four members. Three members and a minority Chair provided a way to balance the interests of the major parties while four spread the workload. One of the important roles of the PAC is to comment on the Auditor-General's draft programme of performance audit work and to seek comment on the programme from the other standing committees. Issues that are seen to pose particular risk for the public sector can be indentified and communicated. This requires an effective working partnership with a well-resourced and capable Auditor-General.

Securing member participation was not such a problem because the PAC was considered both important and prestigious in the ACT Assembly. However, it was important to maintain that prestige and remind ministers and other members that the committee acted for the assembly. Therefore, even small issues such as when a meeting will be scheduled were the prerogative of the PAC. This kind of sensitivity and the management of PAC work are also dependent on an experienced Secretary/Clerk who has a good understanding of the nature and role of the PAC.

While it is a very small jurisdiction, the ACT is relatively well resourced and well developed. The notion of a three-member PAC with an independent Chair is an interesting proposal within a very small jurisdiction and may provide one way to bypass the risk of gridlock in a two-party system. The emphasis on the working relationship with the Auditor-General and the centrality of risk is also an important strategy. However, the key lesson is that the status and prestige of the committee is not inevitable or secure and requires a careful and ongoing work of education and communication.

CONCLUSIONS

PACs in small and developing countries face particular problems and challenges. While some of these are similar, relating to issues of resourcing, there are also differences. There is really not one simple solution. However, in some settings, it may be necessary to deviate from generally accepted ideas to ensure that necessary training and expertise is available both within the membership and within the support staff.

While PACs as small as three members do exist, best practice would recommend between four and ten people. There does not seem to be a clear advantage in having a large membership or large staff numbers. When resources are constrained, the working relationship with the Auditor-General becomes even more critical. In these settings, it is important that a PAC does not face a backlog but they (and the Auditor-General) prioritise their work around areas, controls, or programmes that are deemed to be high risk. Where possible, a joint committee that functions across all Houses of Parliament appears to be best, and a close working relationship between the PAC and other policy review committee seems to be an effective use of limited resources.

However, any and all arrangements need to be designed to respect local processes and arrangements and thereby most effectively deliver good governance and oversight for the good of the country. These small and developing countries illustrate that the ideal model is too simple, a theme that is further explored in the next chapter, which introduces the changing world of PACs.

BIBLIOGRAPHY

McGee, D. 2002. *The Overseers: Public Accounts Committees and Public Spending*, Commonwealth Parliamentary Association and Pluto Press, London.

Stapenhurst, R., Sahgal, V., Woodley, W. and Pelizzo, R. 2005. *Scrutinising Public Expenditure. Assessing the Performance of Public Accounts Committees*, World Bank Policy Research Working Paper 3613, World Bank Institute, Washington DC.

7
The Changing World of PACs

INTRODUCTION

In 2007, Yamamoto[26] wrote a comprehensive report on the distribution of oversight tools in the world. Paying considerable attention to how financial and budgetary oversight is performed, he suggested that such oversight can be performed by one of two types of legislative committees: the finance and budget committee, usually found outside the (British) Commonwealth, and the Public Accounts Committee (PAC), usually found inside the Commonwealth. In his analysis, Yamamoto suggested that PACs only operate in Commonwealth countries, that they play no role whatsoever in the preparation, evaluation, and drafting of the budget, and that they only oversee the implementation of the budget on the basis of the reports submitted to the PAC by the Audit Office.

In recent years, however, a considerable body of research has challenged these generalisations. PACs have been established outside the Commonwealth in countries with no British colonial legacy such as Thailand or Indonesia, a far-from-negligible number/percentage of PACs consider the budget, and nearly three quarters of the PACs for which data have been collected no longer rely solely on Audit Office reports to determine their work but have the unconditional right/power to self-initiate their own inquiries.

26. Using the data that had already been used by Pelizzo and Stapenhurst (2004a, 2004b).

THE CHANGING WORLD OF PACs

This chapter overviews the changing world of PACs – a theme that emerged quite clearly from the Study Group held in Victoria and corroborated by the data collected by Commonwealth Parliamentary Association (CPA) in collaboration with the World Bank Institute (WBI).

In this chapter, we first present a reprise of Chapter 2. We note that the traditional model of the PAC was a peculiarity of the Westminster system and was traditionally found in countries of the (British) Commonwealth, where it oversaw the expenditure of public money. In the second section, we present the new and non-Commonwealth PACs. In doing so, we note that these PACs have emerged in virtually all regions of the world and are now operating under diverse circumstances, including at any level of development and at any level of institutionalisation. Building on this discussion, in the third section, we discuss the role and the functioning of the new PACs and, in so doing, we point out that the new PACs depart in significant ways from the traditional model. In particular, they have a more-active or less-passive/reactive behaviour and are increasingly involved in ex ante oversight. In the fourth section, we compare and contrast 'new' and 'old' PACs. In so doing, we show that they both depart from the traditional model and that, in spite of the fact that they have a different age and operate under different circumstances, they resemble one another. In other words, the changes in the world of PACs are such that the traditional model no longer provides an adequate or accurate depiction/description of what contemporary PACs look like. This point is reiterated in the discussion section where we formulate some conjectures as to why PACs have changed over the years. More importantly, we provide a cautionary note. While we are describing how PACs have changed, and there is no doubt from the data analyses and from the comments expressed in the Study Group that PACs *have* changed, we make it clear that the available evidence and the data at our disposal provide no indication of whether and how these transformations will increase or reduce the effectiveness of PACs. Before concluding, we briefly review an issue that must be unique to PACs – the maintenance of PACs by military or other regimes in the absence of a functioning Parliament. And finally, in the concluding section, we draw some tentative conclusions and raise some questions that will have to be addressed in future research projects.

THE TRADITIONAL PAC MODEL

Public Account Committees have traditionally been associated with a 'Westminster' or a 'Commonwealth' modus operandi, even though the first PAC was established in Denmark (see Box 7.1). Because of the British archetype, PACs have traditionally been found in countries whose national institutions were, at least initially, inherited from the United Kingdom. This 'Commonwealth institutional constellation' has ordinarily included a: (1) common law legal system, (2) parliamentary form of government, and (3) plurality electoral system. Even though many of the United Kingdom's former colonies have subsequently modified their institutional configuration since independence (e.g., many Anglophone African countries now have presidential forms of government), virtually all have retained their PACs.

A second characteristic or peculiarity of the traditional PACs was that they were, for the most part, a reactive institution. They were not involved or consulted in the drafting of the budget, they did not perform any kind of ex ante oversight of the budget estimates, they did not generally have the power to initiate their own investigations, they often lacked the power to instruct the Auditor-General, and they generally acted in response to reports that the Auditor-General tabled.

Some PACs seem to have retained the features that characterised the traditional PAC. In the course of the proceedings of the Study Group, it was pointed out that, in Trinidad and Tobago, the PAC is not terribly active in the sense that it lacks the legal authority to launch its own inquiries, investigations, and

Box 7.1: Denmark's PAC

The first Danish Constitution of 1849 outlined the mandate and authority of the PAC, which was formerly established two years later in 1851. It thus precedes the Westminster PAC by a decade. The primary tasks of the PAC were at that time, and still are:

- To verify that all revenue is correctly reflected in the accounts and that all expenditure has been paid in accordance with legislation
- To verify that the accounts are correct
- To assess whether public funds have been managed properly, and
- To submit the audited public accounts for parliamentary approval

As in most Commonwealth countries, the PAC co-operates closely with the Auditor-General. In Denmark, the PAC has the authority to request specific audit investigations be carried out by the Auditor-General. Audit reports and investigation memoranda from the Auditor-General form the basis of the work of the work of the PACs, although the PAC also has the authority to conduct investigations on its own behalf. Unlike most Commonwealth PACS, however, the Danish PAC has the authority to audit companies and partnerships in which the state or a state-financed institution is a responsible partner. Such investigations may be carried out irrespective of the accounting and auditing regulations that may apply.

The PAC makes the nomination for appointment and dismissal of the Auditor-General to the Speaker of Parliament who, after negotiating with the deputy speakers, presents the nomination to the Standing Orders Committee. (If the nomination cannot be approved, the Speaker notifies the PAC, who then presents a new nomination. In this case, the PAC may request that the post be re-advertised.)

A unique feature of the Danish PAC is that it is *not* a parliamentary committee and there is no requirement that its members be

▶

> Members of Parliament. The Danish Parliament elects six members based on proportional representation, with each major party being represented in the PAC. The Chair is the longest serving member of the committee. Currently, there are six members of the PAC, of which three are MPs. Members are paid and their tenure is four years (which is not affected by general elections). Because the PAC is not a parliamentary committee, the Finance Committee formally presents the accounts to Parliament.
>
> Source: The Public Accounts Committee of the Danish Parliament (2009); *Relations Between Supreme Audit Institutions and Parliamentary Committees* (SIGMA Papers no. 33, 2002).

activities. Participants were told that it can act only on the basis of, or in response to, a report submitted by the Auditor-General, and it lacks the authority to instruct the Auditor-General to launch an investigation or to submit a report.

Many of the Study Group participants confirmed at least some of these characteristics in their own PACs, especially with regard to not playing a role in the drafting or the making of the budget. For instance, the participants from Bhutan, Denmark, India, and Liberia pointed out that their PACs have no role to play in the formulation of the national budget in their country.

The evidence provided by the participants sustains the claim that, in some respects, PACs still retain some of the peculiarities that characterised the traditional PAC. But in other respects, PACs have significantly departed from the traditional PAC such that it is appropriate to speak of the changing world of PACs. This world has changed because of the interaction of three simultaneous transformations: the emergence of new and non-Commonwealth PACs, the emergence of new role and functioning of these PACs, and the changing role and functioning of the old PACs. We consider each in turn.

THE FIRST TRANSFORMATION: THE EMERGENCE OF THE NEW AND NON-COMMONWEALTH PACs

The first and most noticeable change in the world of PAC concerns their distribution. While PACs were once found exclusively in countries of the Commonwealth, now PACs or their functional equivalent are found in several non-Commonwealth countries. The list of countries that have established such committees can be found in Table 7.1.

A cursory glance at the list presented in Table 7.1 makes it clear that PACs (or their functional equivalent) are now found in a very heterogeneous set of countries. The countries listed display great variation in terms of socio-economic development and economic performance, political development and democratic consolidation, and, of course, in terms of geographic location and historical background.

In the sample we find African (Ethiopia, Liberia, Rwanda, South Sudan), Middle Eastern (Afghanistan, Israel, Turkey), South East Asian (Indonesia and Thailand), Asian (Bhutan, Nepal), Pacific (Federated States of Micronesia), and European (Denmark, Finland and Kosovo) countries. We find established

Table 7.1: Non-Commonwealth/new PACs

Afghanistan[27]	Kosovo
Bhutan	Liberia[30]
Denmark[28]	Nepal
Ethiopia[29]	Rwanda
Federated States of Micronesia	Southern Sudan
Finland	Thailand
Israel	Turkey
Indonesia	

27. At the time of writing, Afghanistan's and Turkey's PACs were not operational.
28. As it will be quite clear from the Box 7.1, we are aware of the fact that, while the PAC in Denmark can legitimately regarded as a non-Commonwealth PAC, it is not a new one.
29. On the Ethiopian PAC, see Mengistu (2011).
30. On the Liberian PAC, see Siakor (2011).

or rather consolidated democracies (Denmark) along with third-wave democracies (Indonesia), large countries (Indonesia) along with small ones (Micronesia), 'old' countries (Thailand) and very new ones (South Sudan). In other words, PACs can now be found nearly everywhere, and one may well wonder why a parliamentary committee that was originally created in the United Kingdom for a particular purpose in the mid-nineteenth century has been adopted in so many non-Commonwealth countries.

But while many explanations may be invoked to explain the diffusion of the PAC well beyond the borders of the Commonwealth, this diffusion itself represents the most compelling evidence of its success.[31] Regardless of location, history, tradition, culture, and form of government, many countries have decided to adopt a PAC because the PAC is believed to be one of the most appropriate tools to oversee the expenditure of public money, keep governments accountable for their expenditures, and contribute to the enforcement of the principles of good governance.

THE SECOND TRANSFORMATION: A NEW ROLE AND MODUS OPERANDI OF 'NEW' AND 'NON-COMMONWEALTH' PACs

As Yamamoto (2007) underlined in his comparative analyses, traditional PACs were passive and reactive institutions that could act only in response to a report of the Auditor-General, that generally could not launch their own investigations, that had

31. Various explanations have been proposed to explain the adoption or adaptation of PACs in non-Commonwealth countries. In some instances, it was argued that institutional reformers adopted this type of parliamentary committee for cosmetic purposes, that is to give voters the impression that the political system was really concerned about accountability and good governance. In other cases, it was argued that the adoption or local adaptation of these committees represented a response to the legitimacy crisis of the political system and institutions and represented an attempt to rebuild citizen trust. In other cases, it was suggested that the adoption of a PAC reflected a genuine desire to ensure accountability and good governance. For a comprehensive review of these and additional explanations, see Pelizzo and Stapenhurst (2012).

little power to instruct the Auditor-General as to what should be investigated, and that were generally uninvolved in the preparation of the budget. But while this characterisation is fairly accurate with regard to the traditional PACs, it is remarkably less accurate with regard to the new PACs.

A survey administered by the CPA in collaboration with the WBI collected information from 58 Parliaments in the world, five of which (Bhutan, Indonesia, Kosovo, Nepal, and Thailand) are new PACs. The information collected from these five new PACs allows us to assess whether and to what extent the functioning of the new PACs resembles that of the old PACs, or whether the PACs, while being adopted, were also adapted to local circumstances and hence modified.

The data, presented in Table 7.2, shows that the new PACs depart from the traditional model in significant ways. All of the new PACs have the unconditional power to refer matters for consideration to the Auditor-General, four (Indonesia, Kosovo, Nepal and Thailand) of them have the unconditional power to initiate their own investigation, and one of them (Nepal) reported to have the unconditional power to consider the budget estimates.

In other words, the new PACs do not need to wait for the Auditor-General to submit a report. They can play a much more active role, they can bring matters to the attention of the Auditor-General. and they can initiate their own inquiries. Furthermore, some PACs (Nepal) now have the power to consider the budget estimates. This means that the new PACs perform their oversight function both ex ante and ex post – and, insofar as they consider the budget estimates, refer matters, and launch their own inquiries, they depart from the traditional PAC model described so aptly by Yamamoto (2007).

This evidence sustains the claim that, while the PAC has been adopted outside the Commonwealth, it has undergone a transformation – it has acquired new powers, it has become more active, and it has become a tool of ex ante oversight.

In light of this evidence, one may be tempted to conclude that, while PACs were adopted, they were also adapted. So while it is true that several non-Commonwealth countries now have a PAC or its functional equivalent, it is also undisputable that the features of these newly established committees are quite different from the features displayed by traditional PACs. But drawing such a conclusion would be a mistake.

Table 7.2: Powers of the new PACs

Country	Power to refer matters to the AG	Power to self-initiate an inquiry	Power to consider budget estimates
Bhutan	Yes	No	No
Indonesia	Yes	Yes	No
Kosovo	Yes	Yes	No
Nepal	Yes	Yes	Yes
Thailand	Yes	Yes	No

THE THIRD TRANSFORMATION: THE NEW ROLE AND MODUS OPERANDI OF THE 'OLD' PACs

The third change that has transformed the world of PAC concerns the transformation of the old PACs that have themselves considerably departed from the traditional model.

Table 7.3 presents data on the power to refer matters to the Auditor-General. It can be seen that, while all of the new PACs have this power, in the rest of the world, this power is enjoyed unconditionally by 41 out of the 50 countries (82 percent) for which data were available. Another four PACs (8 percent) reported that they enjoy this power conditionally. In other words, 45 out of 50 Commonwealth PACs (90 percent) reported that their PAC either conditionally or unconditionally enjoys this power.

This evidence sustains the claim that, with regard to the power of referral, the departure of the new PACs from the traditional model is significantly more marked than the departure of the old PACs from tradition, but the data make it quite clear that the overwhelming majority of PACs, regardless of whether they are new or old, now depart from the traditional PAC.

Table 7.3: Power of referral

Number of cases (% of valid responses)

	New PACs	Old PACs	All PACs
No	0	5 (10%)	5 (9.1%)
Yes, conditionally	0	4 (8%)	4 (7.3)
Yes, unconditionally	5 (100%)	41 (82%)	46 (83.6%)
Valid responses	5	50	55
System missing	53	8	3
Total responses	58	58	58

We noted above that the new PACs depart from the traditional model in a second respect. They are more active in the sense that in addition to referring matters to the Auditor-General, and they can also launch their own investigations. In this respect, we observed that 80 percent of the new PACs have the power to conduct self-initiated inquiries.

Table 7.4: Power of self-initiating an inquiry

Number of cases (% of valid responses)

	New PACs	Old PACs	All PACs
No	1 (20%)	12 (28.5%)	13 (27.6%)
Yes, conditionally	0	0	0
Yes, unconditionally	4 (80%)	30 (71.5%)	34 (72.4%)
Valid responses	5	42	47
System missing	53	16	11
Total responses	58	58	58

The data presented in Table 7.4, however, make it clear that this power is also enjoyed unconditionally by 30 out of 42 old PACs (71.5 percent) and that, once we combine the responses of old and new PACs, 34 out of 47 (72.4 percent) of all the PACs enjoy this power.

Finally, in our discussion of the new PAC,s we point out that about 20 percent (1 out of 5) of the new PACs also perform ex ante oversight by considering the budget estimates. The data presented in Table 7.5 make it clear that the new PACs are not terribly exceptional in this respect. In fact, 20 percent of the old PACs (10 out of 50) also consider budget estimates, and 20 percent of all (the old and new) PACs (11 out of 55) consider budget estimates. Further details can be found in Table 7.5.

Table 7.5: Power to consider budget estimates

Number of cases (% of valid responses)

	New PACs	Old PACs	All PACs
No	4 (80%)	40 (80%)	44 (80%)
Yes, conditionally	0	0	0
Yes, unconditionally	1 (20%)	10 (20%)	11 (20%)
Valid responses	5	50	55
System missing	53	8	3
Total responses	58	58	58

DISCUSSION

The data presented in this chapter highlights that the world of PACs has changed in three significant respects. First of all, PACs are no longer confined to the (British) Commonwealth but can now be found in various countries in virtually all regions of the world – regardless of their history, institutional structure, level of socio-economic development, and political development.

The second change is represented by the fact that the emergence or adoption of PACs (or their functional equivalent) around the world has gone hand in hand with a transformation of the functioning of the PACs themselves.

PACs that had traditionally been found in countries of the Commonwealth to perform ex post oversight of the government expenditures, and to respond to and act on the reports of Auditor-

General can now launch their own investigations, they can refer matters to the Auditor-General, and they can consider the budget estimates. In other words, in contrast to the traditional PAC, the new PACs are more active and oversee both ex post and ex ante.

The correlation between the emergence/adoption of such committees outside the Commonwealth may lead one to think that the process of adopting the PAC went along with a process of adapting it to local circumstances. And to some extent, this is precisely what happened. But the data illustrate quite clearly that PACs underwent some significant changes in countries where they were adopted ex novo and adapted to new circumstances, but that they also changed in countries where they had long been in existence. PACs are more likely to refer matters for investigation, to launch their own investigations, and to perform ex ante oversight regardless of whether they are new or old. The traditional model, discussed by Yamamoto (2007), no longer provides an adequate description of the characteristics, the features, and the modus operandi of PACs – regardless of whether they are old or new.

In addition to the changes in the world of PACs revealed by the data analysis, the participants in the Study Group underlined the existence and importance of an additional change – a transformation in the ways PACs understand themselves and their mission. In the words of one of the participants:

> 'I see a development from an understanding of their old role – from discovering fraud, discovering bad management, punishing the people who are responsible – into a new role, where they see themselves having a mission to assist the responsible minister to improve his budget execution and performance. Also, and on a very high level, they see themselves as having the task of guaranteeing to the taxpayers that they could actually trust the execution of the budget.'

Neither the data nor the discussion held in the course of the Study Group allows us to formulate any conjectures as to whether this change in mentality has occurred only in some jurisdictions but not in others or whether it has occurred everywhere. Nor do the data allow us to speculate as to whether the transformations discussed will make PAC work more or less effectively. While one may see greater PAC activism as a positive transformation, one is left to wonder whether granting PACs the power to consider the budget estimates may lead to greater effectiveness of the oversight activities or whether the expansion of the workload of PACs will instead undermine their effectiveness. While one should not confuse the workload of individual MPs with the workload of the PAC, all the participants in our Study Group have lamented that workload – individual and collective – may be detrimental to the proper functioning of the PAC. This view is consistent with what Sartori (1987) argued in his analysis of legislative functions – that, after a certain point, there is an inverse relationship between the amount and the effectiveness – which means that, when a legislature oversees everything, it is no longer able to oversee effectively. The comments and the observations voiced by the participants seem to indicate that Sartori's argument could be applied to the case of PACs.

'AD HOC' PACs

A further, if somewhat unusual, body of evidence for the usefulness of PACs in holding governments to account is the establishment of 'ad hoc' or 'interim' PACs – that is, of an extra-parliamentary PAC. In various Commonwealth countries, including Bangladesh, Fiji, Nigeria, and Pakistan, such committees have been established by the executive arm of government, even in the absence of a functioning parliament. The primary purpose of the ad hoc arrangements is 'to have an interim mechanism for ensuring some continuity of the workings of the Public Accounts Committee during extended periods reflecting abeyance of normal parliamentary proceedings' (Karim, 2012, p. 2).

One of the first such PACs was established in Bangladesh in 1983 by the President through an Ordinance dated 3 November

1983. Justice A. K. Baker was appointed Chair and other members of the committee were drawn from different fields, including the accounting profession, business, civil society, and the army. This committee submitted three reports to the President, reviewing the audit reports relating to FY 1978 and FY 1979. According to Sahgal (2009, p. 1), 'this mechanism not only furthered the financial and legislative scrutiny process but reportedly helped set into motion improved practices that were subsequently adopted by the PACs appointed by [subsequent] incoming Bangladeshi parliaments'.

In Pakistan, the Ad-Hoc Public Accounts Committee (AHPAC) was established in pursuance of the Proclamation of an Emergency in October 1999. While the Chief Executive of the country was appointed with sufficient powers to govern the country, it was determined that an AHPAC was needed to receive and review the audit reports of the Auditor-General and to report to the Chief Executive. Sahgal (2009, p. 1) reported that the committee 'worked diligently and was able to complete its work [including the backlog of Auditor-General reports from previous years] by July 2001'. Interestingly, the committee constituted different sub-committees and inter-departmental committees – practices later noted by McGee (2002) as 'good international practice' for parliamentary PACs to consider. Of particular note is that the proceedings of the AHPAC were opened to the public and the media with the aim of increasing public 'confidence on issues involving accountability and public interest' (Sahgal, 2009, p. 2).

More recently, another attempt was made to establish an interim PAC in Bangladesh. With the dissolution of the eighth Parliament on 27 October 2006, the PAC was dissolved, suspending all its activities. The new Parliament was supposed to be formed following the 22 January 2007 general elections, which were stalled as a result of a political crisis. The Auditor-General asked the caretaker government in July 2007 to constitute an interim PAC to scrutinise the accounts of the government and Auditor-General reports in absence of Parliament. The Auditor-General said that the interim committee would continue its functions until formation of the next Parliament, thereby paving the way for formation of a new, regular PAC. In line with previous national and international experiences, it was recommended that the interim committee consist of a group of distinguished citizens, including former justices, former government officials, academics, and politicians. The Auditor-General highlighted issues such as decisions relating to the recovery of money due to the exchequer and the prompt settlement of other financial irregularities pointed out by audit as important work to be undertaken by the interim PAC (Karim, 2012).

Karim (2012, p. 2) also notes, in a letter sent in June 2007 to the secretary of Parliament Secretariat, that the World Bank highlighted the need for a mechanism such as an interim PAC to ensure the continuity of the PAC's work. The letter further implied that future recommendations emanating from an interim PAC would provide an additional opportunity for the caretaker government to further strengthen the arrangements for good governance and effectiveness of government programmes and activities.

Karim (2012) noted that, while the interim PAC was formed in December 2007 and headed by the then legal adviser to the caretaker government, Mainul Hosein, the committee never got off the ground. Officials from the Auditor-General's office objected to the inclusion of incumbent government secretaries as members of the committee. Strong objections were also raised from the Speaker of the previous Parliament about the very legality of the committee. The Chair of the committee resigned in January 2008 and, sensing that the committee could not be effective due to the legal debate, the Ministry of Finance also did not move to reconstitute the committee following the resignation of its Chair. Thus, the second interim PAC of Bangladesh was scrapped quietly by the caretaker government in June 2008 through a notification that cancelled the Ministry of Finance circular that had declared the formation of the body.

Karim (2012) also reported that the caretaker government assessed alternative arrangements such as commissioning a high-powered advisory committee for the interim period. Such a committee – whose formation was also supported by the World Bank – would also assist the PAC under the next parliament to ease backlog of reports from the Auditor-General's office.

CONCLUSIONS

The world of PACs has changed in significant ways over the years and especially in the course of the past decade. Since the publication of McGee's (2002) classic work, new PACs have been set up in several countries with no institutional legacy from the Westminster model. New PACs have been set up in nearly every continent, in long-established countries and in new ones, in developed ones and in developing ones, in parliamentary systems and in presidential ones.

PACs have enjoyed, in the course of the last decade, an unprecedented popularity. They have been set up to oversee the government expenditures, to prevent corruption, to restore public trust in the political system, and to contribute to the pacification of post-conflict society.

The diffusion across regions, forms of government, level of development, and levels of institutionalisation represents the first transformation in the world of PACs. Indeed, the importance of PACs is underscored by a particularly unusual development – the formation of ad hoc PACs even in the absence of a functioning Parliament.

The emergence of new, non-Commonwealth PACs was coupled with a transformation of the modus operandi of these committees. Originally set up to perform ex post oversight and act upon the reports submitted by the Audit Office, the new PACs have a more active approach: they instruct the Auditor-General, they launch their own investigations and, less commonly, they perform some ex ante oversight activities. In contrast to the traditional model of PAC, the new PACs do not simply focus on scrutinising the expenditures of the executive ex post, but they are also tasked with considering budget estimates. Interestingly, even older PACs have changed – they are more active and perform their oversight tasks both ex post and ex ante.

The evidence at our disposal does not provide any indication of whether and how these changes will affect the effectiveness of PACs. If the effectiveness of PACs is simply a function of the breadth of their terms of reference, the changes discussed in this chapter should translate, sooner or later, into greater oversight effectiveness. If the effectiveness of PACs is inversely related to the amount of activities that they are asked to perform, then the expansion of PACs' terms of reference may be a subtle solution for preventing PACs and legislatures from effectively performing their oversight function.

Future studies will have to provide a more compelling answer as to whether the expansion of PACs' mandate was a way to make them work better or not to make them work at all.

BIBLIOGRAPHY

Karim, S. 2012. 'Interim PACs in Bangladesh' (unpublished report).
McGee, D. 2002. *The Overseers: Public Accounts Committees and Public Spending*, Commonwealth Parliamentary Association and Pluto Press, London.
Mengistu, M. 2011. 'Strengthening Financial Accountability and Parliamentary Oversight in the Federal Republic of Ethiopia', in Stapenhurst, F., Draman, R., Imlach, A., Hamilton, A. and Kroon, C. (eds), *Africa Parliamentary Reform*, pp. 70–80, Routledge, London.
Pelizzo, R. and Stapenhurst, F. 2004a. 'Legislatures and Oversight: A Note', *Quaderni di scienza politica*, vol. 11, no. 1, pp. 175–88.
Pelizzo, R. and Stapenhurst, F. 2004b. 'Tools for Legislative Oversight: An Empirical Investigation', World Bank Policy Research Working Paper no. 3388, World Bank Institute, Washington DC.
Pelizzo, R. and Stapenhurst, F. 2012. *Parliamentary Oversight Tools*, Routledge, London.
Sahgal, V. 2009. 'PACs – Even in the Absence of Parliament' (unpublished report).
Sartori, G. 1987. *Elementi di Teoria Politica*, Il Mulino, Bologna.

Siakor, F. 2011. 'Rebuilding Parliament in a Conflict-Affected Country', in Stapenhurst, F., Draman, R., Imlach, A., Hamilton, A. and Kroon, C. (eds), *Africa Parliamentary Reform*, pp. 81–2, Routledge, London.

Yamamoto, H. 2007. *Tools for Parliamentary Oversight. A Comparative Study of 88 National Parliaments*, IPU, Geneva.

8
The Political Will for Parliamentary Oversight

INTRODUCTION

Chapter 3 highlights the structural differences between Public Accounts Committees (PACs) in different countries and suggests that there is not a simple relationship between structural characteristics and PAC performance. Chapter 4 extends this argument to explore the relationship between PAC activity and performance. While there are some clear links between activity and PAC performance, one of the key issues is the difference between an active PAC where there is a strong political will to support good governance and parliamentary oversight and other jurisdictions where there is not that same level of political will to support robust and critical oversight to the point that the actions of the executive might be subject to public criticism. This distinction suggests that further work is required to explore the question of why (or why not) there is the political will for this kind of oversight in some settings and not others and the link between a notion of political will and PAC effectiveness.

For the past five years or so, scholars and practitioners alike have struggled to detect any meaningful relationship between oversight capacity and oversight effectiveness, and have wondered whether their inability to detect such a relationship should be attributed to methodological reasons (capacity and effectiveness are not adequately measured) or to the fact that what drives oversight effectiveness is political will to use the oversight tools and not the oversight tools at the disposal of a legislature.

The first approach, espoused by the Parliamentary Centre (Draman, forthcoming; Parliamentary Centre, 2011), the Commonwealth Parliamentary Association (2006), the National Democratic Institute (2007), and Stapenhurst (2011), holds that we need to develop better measures. The second approach, espoused by Ebo and N'Diaye (2008), APPG (2008), and Pelizzo and Stapenhurst (2012), holds that political will is the single most important determinant of legislative oversight effectiveness – in doing so this approach introduced a voluntaristic element that was overlooked by all the other approaches.[32]

Pelizzo and Stapenhurst (2012) suggested a third approach – that we need better measures and that we need to look *beyond* capacity. They argued that there is a portion of oversight effectiveness that cannot be explained on the basis of the number of tools available to a legislature, of the presence/absence of specific institutions that may assist a legislature in its oversight tasks, and of other facilitating conditions. The explanation for this portion of the variance must be found beyond capacity, in the willingness of legislatures and legislators to effectively perform their oversight tasks. This point was underscored by members of the Commonwealth Parliamentary Association–World Bank Institute (CPA-WBI) Study Group, who highlighted the importance of what was alternatively called political will or attitude, but who also shed some light as to the conditions under

---

32. In their exploration of what is responsible for the effectiveness of the oversight process, Pelizzo and Stapenhurst (2012) suggest that political will is an essential prerequisite for translating or transforming oversight capacity into oversight effectiveness. They underlined that oversight capacity and oversight effectiveness are not the same thing and pointed out that while oversight capacity was measured on the basis of oversight tools at the disposal of the legislature, oversight effectiveness was measured on the basis of a variable included in the Polity IV dataset – a variable that tracks whether and to what extent the executive's actions are subject to some constraints.

which such a political will is most likely to emerge. Parliamentary committees have an interest in effectively overseeing the actions of the executive. This proposition can be reformulated in a more cogent form. Since we know that the oversight process can generate a plurality of outcomes (disclosure of information, modification of legislation, disciplinary action, legal action, increase in the level of legitimacy enjoyed by the legislature, and so on), we can say that a legislature effectively engages in an oversight activity when it has the reasonable expectation of deriving a benefit (material, symbolic or otherwise) from one or more of the outcomes that the oversight process can generate.

There are, however, times when a legislature may not have the political will to oversee the executive, times when a legislature is noted more for its acquiescence than for its determination to keep the government accountable. In these instances, when legislators refrain from performing in even a minimally acceptable way their oversight role, they do not have the will to effectively oversee the executive because they believe that they may gain more, individually and collectively, from being ineffective overseers than from being effective overseers.

In other words, the presence/absence of a political will reflects the structure of incentives confronting legislators. The implication is that, if the structure of incentives changes, a legislature that was previously content of avoiding its constitutionally mandated oversight tasks may find plenty of incentives to engage in effective oversight of the executive. But how can the structure of incentives be modified? This is what we now discuss.

As soon as voters demand that the government be held accountable for its actions, decisions, policies, and expenditures, the structure of incentives shifts: it becomes immediately rewarding for legislators to engage in effective oversight and oversee the government actions. This means that it is sufficient to generate or stimulate voter demands for accountability in order to ensure that oversight activities will be effectively performed by the legislature. If voters demand more-effective oversight and are willing to reward effective overseers for their oversight activity, there are clear benefits that legislators can derive from effectively performing the oversight function.

In this chapter, we present a strategic interaction model, which includes at its centre how and why political will impacts the effectiveness of PACs.

STRATEGIC INTERACTION MODEL

In 2012, Pelizzo and Stapenhurst developed a model to incorporate political will and dynamic change into the analysis of PACs and legislative oversight (see Figure 8.1). In that model, there were two sets of actors: the members of the ruling elite and the members of society. Whether an institutional reform occurs or a newly established institution succeeds depends on the interaction of these two groups. The alleged mismanagement of public resources, for example, may erode the legitimacy of the ruling elite and of the political system. In response, citizens and social groups may voice their discontent with the functioning of the political system and they may demand political reforms and institutional changes to eliminate the problems that the crisis disclosed.

The ruling elite, confronted with these popular demands, faces two options: it may decide to preserve the status quo or it may decide to make some institutional reforms. The ruling elite's decision to reform or not to reform the political system depends on how strong the ruling elite is (or, at least, on how strong it believes to be) and on how strong the ruling believes society and social demands to be. If the ruling elite believe that it is strong enough to neglect social demands without having to pay the price for such a choice, the ruling elite will decide to preserve the status quo. However, if the ruling elite believes that an effort to preserve the status quo may exacerbate the crisis, further delegitimising the ruling class, and potentially leading to more disastrous changes such as civil conflict or military coup, the ruling elite will agree to make some institutional changes.

Furthermore, at this stage, the ruling elite may still be very much convinced that any institutional reform will be purely formal and cosmetic, that it will not amount to any meaningful change, and that it will not produce a substantive change in how the political system operates. Once the ruling elite enacts the institutional reforms, society is left with two basic choices: to regard the reforms as a political success, to be satisfied by what it was able to achieve and drop additional demands, or alternatively to articulate further demands. If society makes the first choice, the reforms are enacted but they are fairly ineffective in tackling the problems for which they had been demanded in the first place. If society makes the second choice, it puts the ruling elite in a very difficult position. In fact, if society demands additional, or more incisive, reforms, the ruling elite is left with three unappealing prospects: to ensure that the newly established reforms perform effectively, in which case the reforms succeed and the ruling elite may lose some of the benefits it had previously enjoyed in the status quo ante; to neglect the new social demands and run the risk of losing whatever legitimacy it has left, thereby creating the conditions for a further crisis; or, finally, to ignore popular demands, tolerate unethical and corrupt behaviour and the suboptimal functioning of the newly established institutions at the risk, once again, of compromising its legitimacy and that of the political system as a whole. The model is presented in Figure 8.1.

The case of Indonesia is emblematic in this respect. The Indonesian political system has historically been ranked as being highly corrupt, and the legislature has been ranked as one of the least trusted institutions in the country (Pelizzo and Ang, 2008). To cope with this legitimacy crisis, the Indonesian parliament reformed its committee system and established a functional analogue to what is a PAC. Its adoption was facilitated, if not caused, by the need to cope with popular demands for good governance exactly as the model suggests.

Broadening the empirical application of the model, in recent years, there have been various efforts to explain the diffusion of PACs outside the Commonwealth. Most notably, Hamilton and

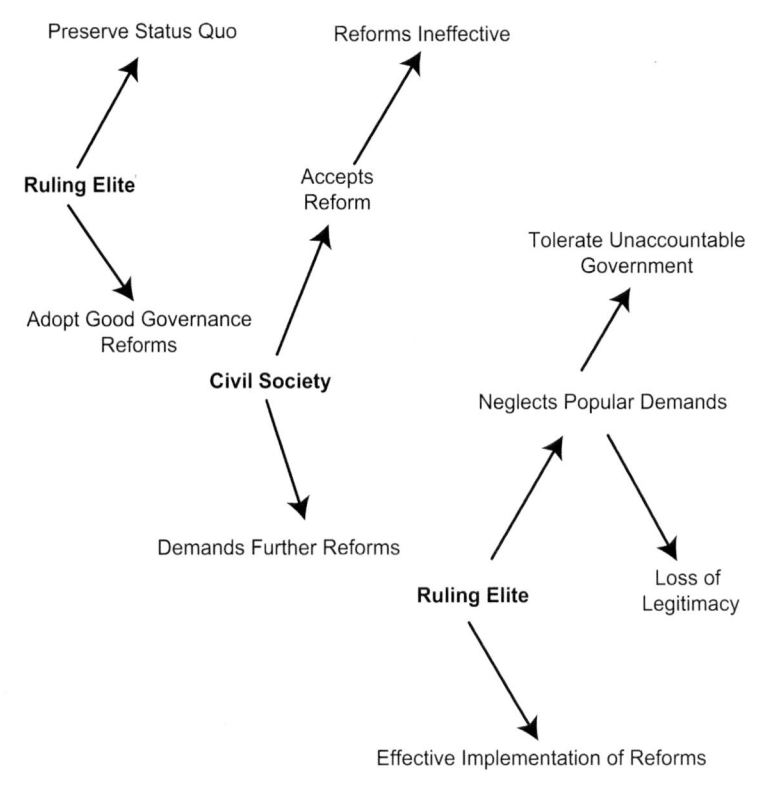

```
Preserve Status Quo      Reforms Ineffective
        ↑                      ↑
       /                      /
      /                      /
**Ruling Elite**        Accepts
      \                 Reform
       \                  ↑
        ↓                /         Tolerate Unaccountable
Adopt Good Governance   /                Government
       Reforms         /                     ↑
                      /                     /
              **Civil Society**            /
                      \              Neglects Popular Demands
                       \                    ↑         \
                        ↓                  /           \
              Demands Further Reforms     /             ↓
                                         /           Loss of
                                  **Ruling Elite**   Legitimacy
                                         \
                                          ↓
                          Effective Implementation of Reforms
```

Figure 8.1: Strategic Interaction Model

Source: Pelizzo and Stapenhurst (2012).

Stapenhurst (2011) tested whether the diffusion of the PAC could be explained on the basis of three theoretical frameworks – an historical one, a rational choice one, and a sociological one. They found that historical legacies matter little in determining whether a country adopts a PAC or not and that, structurally and organisationally, the PACs established outside the Commonwealth resemble fairly closely the PACs that operate in the countries in the Commonwealth. However, Hamilton and Stapenhurst (2011) were unable to demonstrate that PACs work equally well inside and outside the Commonwealth; the relationship between the organisational and structural characteristics of PACs do not have a deterministic impact on the amount of activities performed by these committees or on whether such activities are carried out efficiently and effectively.

The strategic interaction model explains this. It does not assume that actors (ruling elite or civil society groups) act in the vacuum, nor does it assume that the preferences/choices/ strategies of these actors are fixed over time. Rather, it makes it clear that political actors interact in a dynamic way by constantly modifying their behaviour and strategy in response to what is done by their counterparts. Furthermore, it explains something that neither the rational choice theorists nor the sociological-institutionalist theorists are able to explain; namely, why for a long time ruling elites had little interest in reforming the institutional arrangement by adopting a PAC while at some point they decided to do so.

Of course, one could say that the decision to adopt a PAC could be stimulated by an exogenous stimulus. In such a case, the international community may feel that corruption represents a major obstacle for a country's socio-economic development, makes pressure on that country's political class to take some active steps to curb corruption, and recommends, among other measures, the adoption of a PAC. But if the adoption of a PAC were simply a response to an exogenous stimulus of this kind, PACs should be more widespread than they are and they should be found in all the countries in which international organisations promote anticorruption programmes and activities. Yet, this is far from being the case. Many countries that have high levels of corruption have not felt the need to take significant steps to fight corruption or to adopt a PAC.

Our model can explain why this is the case. A country's political elite is willing to launch a set of institutional reforms only when its survival as ruling class is at risk. It is only when a crisis occurs and the political system is losing legitimacy and needs to take active steps to regain citizen trust that the reforms are enacted. To paraphrase what we wrote earlier (Pelizzo and Stapenhurst,

2006, p. 198), the adaptation of reforms (such as the establishment of a PAC) represents an attempt to rebuild the public trust in the political system. In the absence of such a crisis, reformist pressures from the international community and from civil society will not persuade the ruling class to make any institutional changes.

The claim that reforms (such as the adoption of a PAC) are a response to crises of legitimacy is supported by empirical evidence. Indonesia has recently established a PAC to scrutinise government expenditure, reduce corruption, preserve/improve citizen trust of Parliament, and prevent the delegitimisation of Parliament and of the other democratic institutions. Similarly, in Thailand, where democracy collapsed in 2006 in the midst of a corruption crisis, a PAC has been established to improve the level of governance and create firmer conditions for the consolidation and the survival of the newly established democracy. Much in the same vein, a PAC was created in Ethiopia in 2006 as part of a government attempt to diffuse political tensions that engulfed the country following the 2005 national elections. Specifically, it was established in order to bolster the role of Parliament following allegations over election irregularities and an attempt, by the outgoing Parliament, to weaken the ability of opposition parties to fully participate in parliamentary procedures.

CONCLUSIONS

PACs need a proper mandate and proper resources in order to effectively perform their oversight function. But regardless of how important structural and institutional conditions are, they are not as important as the political will to make an effective use of the oversight capacity and resources with which they are endowed.

Providing the PAC with the capacity of adequate resources, a generous budget, a large number of well-trained staff members, and a wide mandate is necessary but not sufficient to holding the executive accountable for its expenditures. We would argue that what is also required is that the PAC and its members have the political will to refer matters to the Auditor-General, launch investigations, hold hearings, and ask the executive to account for how departments are run and money is spent. Therefore, effective oversight is the result of the combination of oversight capacity and the political will to use it – a theme that has been addressed in the scholarly literature (Pelizzo and Stapenhurst, 2012) and that has been confirmed by the participants who attended the Study Group in Victoria.

One of the issues that provides a challenge to the political will of PACs and parliamentary oversight in general is that the allocation of seats in the various committees tend to reflect the distribution of seats in the legislature. Therefore, the political party (or parties) in government tends also to control the majority of seats in committees such as the PAC and, as the executive face, disincentives against a strong and robust oversight function. PAC members affiliated with the government party face disincentives which can reduce robust oversight. These disincentives include political party discipline, concerns about own political career, desire for re-election, and a general loyalty (or accusations of disloyalty) to their party leadership.

There are two basic solutions for this problem. The first solution is simple: government parties should not be allowed to have a majority of seats on the PAC. The evidence has shown that, when the opposition forces control a majority of seats in the PAC, the PAC works effectively even if it is chaired by an MP affiliated with the government party (Pelizzo, 2011). The second solution consists in generating in government-affiliated MPs the political will to oversee the executive.

Political will can be generated in two ways: either by making an appeal to reason or by making an appeal to self-interest. The appeal to reason reminds MPs that they have a constitutional mandate to oversee the executive. In other words, no matter how unappealing they find the tasks of overseeing the executive and its accounts, they are constitutionally mandated to do so.

The appeal to self-interest is the best strategy to ensure that MPs develop the political will to oversee the executive. Legislators are rational actors in the sense that they adopt rational or at least reasonable strategies to achieve their own objectives They are rational because they adopt what they regard as the most effective means to achieving certain ends. Re-election is the single most important end that all legislators have. Legislators want to be elected and, once in office, they want to be re-elected. Legislators, therefore, choose what to do or not to do, what battles to pick, and what battles to drop on the basis of whether they believe that taking a certain position on an issue or by performing a specific action will increase their chances to be re-elected or not.

If the media provide extensive coverage of the Auditor-General's report and findings and denounce the fact that the PAC is unwilling to hold hearings and carry out an investigation, PAC members can easily be portrayed in a fairly negative way (they are ineffective, they do not do their job, they do not care about how money is spent, they do not care about us …) and this negative portrayal may undermine the chances of being re-elected; whereas if PAC members eagerly perform their oversight task they can be portrayed as the most effective agents of society and may benefit electorally from such positive media coverage.

Hence, the way to induce MPs to develop the political will to oversee the executive consists in showing that, contrary to what they may assume or believe, the effective performance of the oversight function is beneficial for their chances to be re-elected and for their career development.

This conclusion was formally advanced in the literature (Pelizzo and Stapenhurst, 2012). These two scholars suggested that, if the media pay attention to oversight and the voters become concerned with oversight, members of the political elites have two options: either to neglect the voter demands (at the risk of delegitimising themselves and the whole political system) or they can engage in oversight activities and be responsive. If voters are satisfied with this response, the PAC will perform its oversight function only in a very superficial way. If the voters are not satisfied with this response, the PAC will be under some pressure to perform its oversight function effectively because it either performs the oversight function effectively and substantively satisfies voter demands or gives voters the impression of being irresponsive and out of touch with reality (and thus likely suffer a loss of legitimacy and, ultimately, the parliamentary seat).

This conclusion is also supported by empirical evidence. In a number of countries, some Parliamentarians have established themselves as the anti-corruption MPs, as the good-governance MPs, or simply as the effective overseers, and have enjoyed long and successful political careers because of their commitment to oversight, good governance, and aversion to corruption.

Hence, the lesson is: effective oversight provides some with the foundation for launching a successful career in politics, while it provides others with a chance to prolong their political career. It is precisely because legislative oversight can be either a career-prolonging or a career-making activity that MPs should be keen to be or become effective overseers.

BIBLIOGRAPHY

APPG on Africa. 2008. 'Strengthening Parliament in Africa', http://siteresources.worldbank.org/PSGLP/Resources/StrengtheningParliamentsinAfrica.pdf.

Draman, R. forthcoming. 'African Parliamentary Index', in O'Brien, M. (ed.), *Parliamentary Indicators and Benchmarks* (working title), World Bank Institute, Washington DC.

Ebo, A. and N'Diaye, B. (eds). 2008. *Parliamentary Oversight of the security sector in West Africa*, Geneva Centre for the Democratic Control of Armed Forces (DCAF), Geneva.

Stapenhurst, R. and Hamilton, A. 2011. 'The Influence of Commonwealth Parliamentary Public Accounts Committees on non-Commonwealth Parliaments', in *The Evolution of Commonwealth Parliamentary Democracy: The CPA at 100*, Commonwealth Parliamentary Association, London.

National Democratic Institute. 2007. *Toward the Development of International Standards for Democratic Legislatures: A Discussion Document for Review by Interested Legislatures, Donors and International Organizations*, Handbook.

Parliamentary Centre. 2011. *Africa Parliamentary Index. A Report for Seven African Countries*, Parliamentary Centre, Ottawa. www.parlcent.org/en/wp-content/uploads/2011/09/API-African-Parliamentary-Index.pdf.

Pelizzo, R. and Stapenhurst, F. 2006. 'Legislative Ethics and Codes of Conduct', in Stapenhurst, R., Johnston, N. and Pelizzo, R. (eds), *The Role of Parliament in Curbing Corruption*, pp. 197–205, World Bank Institute, Washington DC.

Pelizzo, R. and Stapenhurst, F. 2012. *Parliamentary Oversight Tools*, Routledge, London.

Stapenhurst, F. 2011. 'Legislative Oversight and Corruption: Presidentialism and Parliamentarianism Revisited'. Unpublished thesis. Australian National University, Canberra.

9
A Best Practice Guide for PACs

INTRODUCTION

Following a survey of 33 Public Accounts Committees (PACs) from different jurisdictions around the Commonwealth, in which PAC Chairs were asked to self-assess the impact of the committee's work and to identify important 'success factors' and 'inhibiting factors' affecting PAC performance, Stapenhurst et al. (2005) presented, albeit cautiously, attributes of an ideal PAC. These factors are presented in Box 9.1. These factors have been suggested to different meetings of PACs around the Commonwealth, and there appears to be a general consensus on their validity. Indeed, several national and regional associations of PACs have adopted these factors. Since 2005, two additional major studies have contributed to this initial analysis – Hedger and Blick (2008) developed a framework for analysing PAC effectiveness, and Ngozwana (2009) proposed a set of PAC guidelines for the Southern African Development Community of PACs.

In this chapter, we first review the success factors proposed by Stapenhurst et al. (2005) against the findings presented in this book. Then, we present an updated best practice guide using Stapenhurst et al. (2005), supplemented by Hedger and Bliss (2008) and Ngozwana (2009), as a point of departure, and modifying attributes and benchmarks to reflect the new research findings presented in this book.

ATTRIBUTES OF A SUCCESSFUL PAC

Stapenhurst et al. (2005) proposed a set of attributes that they believed affected PAC performance. We group these under five major headings: mandate and legal powers, relationship with the Auditor-General, structure and internal organisation, activities (practices and procedures), and resources.

Mandate and Legal Powers

Establishment

PACs are established and institutionalised through a country's constitution, an Act of Parliament, or through parliamentary Standing Orders (House Rules).

There is no consensus regarding whether the performance of a PAC is affected by the legislative/normative framework under which it operates. Some scholars and practitioners believe in the unconditional importance of the normative framework under which a PAC operates in shaping its performance; but even here there is no consensus. Rawlings (2005), for example, believes that PACs operate more effectively when they are established by constitutional dispositions and less effectively otherwise, while Jacobs, Jones, and Smith (2007) believe that PACs operate more effectively when they are established by an Act of Parliament.

Others still, such as Hardmann (1984a, 1984b, 1986), have stressed that the relationship between norms and rules on the one hand and performance on the other hand is conditional. Indeed, Hardmann (1986) argued that 'sedulous adherence to conventional Westminster forms and mechanisms in financial legislation on and after self-government ... precluded the emergence of innovatory measures specifically addressing indigenous development and

Box 9.1: An 'ideal committee'

- The committee is small; committees seem to work well with five to eleven members, none of whom should be government ministers.
- Senior opposition figures are associated with the PAC's work, and probably chair the committee.
- The Chair is a senior Parliamentarian, fair-minded, and respected by Parliament.
- The committee is appointed for the full term of the Parliament.
- The committee is adequately resourced, with an experienced clerk and a competent researcher(s).
- There is clarity on the committee's role and responsibilities.
- The committee meets frequently and regularly.
- Hearings are open to the public; a full verbatim transcript and summary minutes are quickly available for public distribution.
- A steering committee plans the committee's work in advance and prepares an agenda for each meeting to the full committee.
- The typical witness is a senior public servant (the 'accounting officer') accompanied by the officials that have detailed understanding of the issues under examination.
- The Auditor's Report is automatically referred to the committee and the auditor meets with the committee to go over the highlights of the report.
- In addition to issues raised by the Auditor, the committee occasionally decides to investigate other matters.
- The committee strives for some consensus in their reports.
- The committee issues formal substantive reports to Parliament at least annually.
- The committee has established a procedure with the government for following up its recommendations and is informed about what, if any, action has been taken.
- In all its deliberations, the committee uses the auditor as an expert adviser.
- Parliaments hold an annual debate on the work of the committee.

Source: Stapenhurst et al. (2005, p. 25).

cultural preservation'. He went on to argue that the financial legislation modelled after that of the former colonial powers was inadequate, that financial control was inefficient, and that more effective financial scrutiny could be provided by developing local solutions to local conditions.

Mandate

Regardless of how constituted, a PAC's mandate can be expressed narrowly by concentrating on financial probity and regularity, or can be expressed more widely in relation to performance or value for money audits. There are few PACs today whose mandate is limited to financial probity – although many PACs are moving to performance and value for money audits without sufficient training or, indeed, sophisticated reports from the Auditor-General. Furthermore, in most countries, the mandate of PACs is limited to ex post scrutiny, investigating whether or not government expenditure complied with Parliament's intention. Because PACs generally do not question the underlying policies that inform public spending, they tend not to undertake ex ante budget scrutiny (i.e., the detailed critical analysis of the government's proposed budget).[34]

In some countries, PACs also perform an ex ante role, which, among others, includes reviewing budget estimates, evaluating the virtues of government policies, and assessing governments' legislative proposals. This would seem to be appropriate for PACs in smaller jurisdictions. However, it has been found that PACs are most effective when they do not assess policies but limit their oversight to the implementation of policy.

With this fundamental disagreement on legislative dispositions, it would seem that the attribute noted by Stapenhurst et al. (2005); namely, that:

- **There is clarity on the committee's role and responsibilities**

34. There are a number of exceptions, though, including New Zealand and the Australian state of Victoria.

presents a lowest common denominator with which few can argue. Ngozwana (2009) drills down and adds several additional benchmarks that the literature generally supports:

- The Rules and/Acts of Parliament must empower the PAC with appropriate powers to carry out its mandate.
- PAC members should have a common understanding and articulation of the PAC's mandate, roles, and powers.
- PAC members must have a good understanding of how PAC powers should be applied.
- The Rules and Acts of Parliament should allow for regular review and updating of PACs' mandate to ensure that it remains adequate and relevant to the current political and legislative context.

Access to information

In our analyses, we found that the mandate relates to two main issues; namely, the access that a PAC had to areas of government and sections of the private sector who use public funds, and the powers that a PAC has to do their work and conduct their investigations. While certain levels of access and certain investigative powers might be regarded as 'normal practice', there were more divergences on both of these issues than might have been expected. In reviewing the mandated right of access, we suggest that most PACs should have a broad access to all government agencies both within and outside of the finance portfolio. Those who have constitutional restrictions in this area should seek to have their mandate extended. Many PACs have also obtained the power to 'follow' government money and investigate government and non-government service providers. PACs should also be encouraged to extend their mandate in this area. Some PACs have oversight for local government activity; this would seem to be a particularly effective approach for small jurisdictions. We therefore propose a new attribute, namely:

- The committee should have unconditional access to all government agencies and have the power to 'follow' government money provided to non-government service providers.

Self-initiated inquiries

There is no clear pattern regarding another important PAC power; namely, to self-initiated inquiries. Nevertheless, Study Group participants endorsed the attribute that:

- In addition to issues raised by the Auditor, the committee has the power to investigate other matters.

Scrutiny of estimates

While again there is no clear pattern regarding the examination of estimates, there is evidence to suggest another new attribute:

- In smaller jurisdictions, there may be benefit in combining ex post and ex ante budget review within the remit of the PAC.

Reporting to Parliament

McGee (2002) noted there is wide variation of PAC reporting in the Commonwealth. In some cases, the PAC issues only one report each year to Parliament on all work on which it has been engaged during the course of that time. In others, PACs report to the legislature as they see fit, and their reports can deal with a number of issues or can relate to a single investigation that the PAC considers warrants communication to the House in a standalone report. Stapenhurst et al. (2005) highlight the importance of reporting publicly, and Study Group members support two of the attributes proposed by Stapenhurst et al. (2005); namely:

- The committee issues formal substantive reports to parliament at least annually;
- Parliament holds an annual debate on the work of the committee.

This latter attribute reflects the fact that the PAC is accountable to, and reports to, Parliament. However, it is the government that is responsible for responding to committee recommendations (KPMG, 2006). While the majority of committee recommendations involve issues of general public and financial administration, it is usually the responsibility of the minister to respond.

Ngozwana (2009) suggests that it may be important to consider some of the following content suggestions for a comprehensive committee report:

- Summary statement of the mandate of the PAC as well as standard procedures and guidelines.
- Description of the work completed in a given period (i.e. issues investigated). Reference should be made to the audit report if issues investigated were raised by the Auditor-General (or respective Supreme Audit Institution – SAI).
- Summary of evidence received from witnesses; (some PACs produce verbatim transcripts of the hearings as a detailed record follow-up in the following year).
- Key findings of the PAC investigations: the key problems identified, the PAC's opinions on the problems, and the conclusions reached.
- Summary of the PAC's recommendations on corrective measures to be undertaken by the government in addressing the problems identified.

Follow-up

Follow-up to committee recommendations is important. While a PAC's recommendations are not binding, it is expected that the government will implement them. In most countries, government is obliged to provide a formal response to a PAC's recommendations within a specified period. A general problem in many countries is government recalcitrance and lack of responsiveness to PAC recommendations (Wehner, 2003). Ascertaining what action has been taken in response to PAC recommendations is an important aspect of measuring a PAC's effectiveness (McGee, 2002). This leads to another attribute initially proposed by Stapenhurst et al. (2005); namely, that:

- **The committee has established a procedure with the government for following up its recommendations and is informed about what, if any, action has been taken.**

Relationship with the Auditor-General

Wehner (2003, page 27) notes that the 'overwhelming majority of PAC work is dedicated with dealing with Auditors General reports ... In the Westminster tradition, the PAC is the principal audience of the Auditor General, and it is vital that a cordial relationship is maintained between the two. While the PAC depends on high quality audit reporting to be effective, the Auditor General in turn requires an effective PAC to ensure that departments take audit outcomes seriously.' Or, as quoted from the Indian Lok Sabha in Stapenhurst et al. (2005 p. 12), the Auditor-General is the PAC's 'friend, philosopher and guide'. Our analysis supports this and the two attributes:

- **The Auditor's Report is automatically referred to the committee and the Auditor meets with the committee to go over the highlights of the report.**
- **In all its deliberations, the committee uses the Auditor as an expert adviser.**

Ngozwana (2009) made some additional suggestions:

- Members should closely review the audit report and pay attention to specific sections of the report that have been flagged by the Auditor-General.

- The Auditor-General should brief the PAC on the contents of the audit report and highlight areas of the report that require special attention. This, however, does not take away the right of the PAC members to assess any other areas they may deem necessary for review. The Auditor-General's briefing of the committee is done verbally, but a briefing note should be used and distributed to all members of the committee beforehand.

Structure and Organisation

Size

One of the key elements of any parliamentary committee is its size. In the majority of countries, the same Rules and Acts of Parliament that provide for an establishment of a PAC also prescribe the size of a PAC's membership. As Chapter 3 shows, both McGee (2002) and Pelizzo (2011) found that the average number of MPs serving on the committee was about 11 — about 11 for McGee and 11.6 for Pelizzo. The 2009 survey presents a very similar picture: the size of a PAC varies from a minimum of 3 MPs to a maximum of 31 MPs, with an average of 10.6. Reflecting these findings, and comments from PAC Chairs, Stapenhurst et al. (2005) proposed the following attribute:

- **The committee is small; committees seem to work well with 5–11 members, none of whom should be government ministers.**

Evidence presented in this book shows that the size of the committee is strongly related to PAC output (the number of meetings, hearings, and completed inquiries) and performance. Ngozwana (2009) proposed some practical issues to consider in determining the size of a PAC:

- The PAC's mandate and responsibilities.

- The size of Parliament.
- The number of audit reports to be reviewed by the PAC.

Political representation

Political representation on the PAC has two dimensions: the party affiliation of the Chair and the proportion of Committee members from opposition parties.

By tradition, in the United Kingdom, the Chair of PAC is a leading member of the Official Opposition. Wehner (2003, p. 27) suggests that 'This gives organizational expression to the non-partisan tradition that underpins the work of PAC, and indicates an intention of parliament to promote transparency through independent scrutiny.' Currently, some 70 per cent of PACs are chaired by a member of the opposition and this is generally accepted as 'good practice' (Ngozwana, 2009). It provides a balancing the power between the government's party – which has a majority of members on the committee – and the opposition, thereby ensuring that the PAC provides meaningful opportunities for the opposition to contribute to effective oversight of budget expenditures. This would seem to support the attributes:

- **Senior opposition figures are associated with the PAC's work, and probably chair the committee.**

Regardless of party affiliation, the Chair is ultimately responsible for the effective operation of the PAC (KPMG, 2006); McGee (2002, p. 66) considered 'what is of first importance is the capacity of the Chair to carry out the duties of the office effectively, rather than whether he or she is drawn from the government or the opposition ranks'. The Chair must demonstrate fair-mindedness and command the respect of Parliament; thus:

- **The Chair is a senior Parliamentarian, fair-minded and respected by Parliament.**

Ngozwana (2009) suggests that a PAC Chair:

- should have strong leadership skills (e.g., competence, firmness, honesty, dependability, objectivity) and be knowledgeable in the matters of PACs,
- should have the ability to articulate the non-partisan objective of the Committee and ensure that members have a shared understanding of this objective,
- should have the ability to manage all the PAC's processes, including meetings and hearings.

Generally, the procedure for appointing a PAC chairperson is standard: a Chair is nominated and elected by the committee members. Should more than one candidate be nominated, the committee members vote and the candidate that wins with simple majority becomes the chairperson.

With regard to the presence of opposition MPs on PACs, McGee (2002) noted that representation in the PAC generally reflects the balance of political power in the legislature, that PACs are not dominated by government parties. In the CPA-WBI Study Group we held in Victoria, several participants underlined the importance of members. Some participants underlined that excessive political fragmentation may be detrimental to the proper functioning of PACs, while others noted that the success of PACs depends almost entirely on the quality of their members – which is why members sitting on PACs need to receive proper training (see below). Our own analysis shows that the representation of opposition parties on the PAC is a critical success factor; thus:

- **Committee membership should provide for adequate participation by opposition MPs; their proportion of PAC membership should at least represent their proportion of the seats in Parliament.**

Members: appointments/term of office

There is no commonly accepted process of appointing PAC members. Ngozwana (2009) notes two main approaches: first, the selection by a Parliamentary Committee of Selection or similar and second being the nomination by political parties represented in Parliament. However they are appointed the selection/nomination process is normally followed by the formal appointment of the members to the PAC by the Parliamentary Speaker.

McGee (2002) noted that in most Commonwealth Parliaments, PAC members are appointed for the term of Parliament, although in some, they serve for shorter periods. He contends that committee effectiveness is promoted by continuity of membership and that, '… in general, longevity of membership will strengthen the PAC' (p. 62). Evidence from the Study Group supports notion that, regardless of how selection occurs, length of term is what makes committees effective.

- **The committee is appointed for the full term of the Parliament.**

Ngozwana (2009) goes further and proposes:

- Experience and continuity are some of the critical factors for success of a PAC.
- The nature of a PAC's work is such that it may carry over from one year to another and may require follow-up.
- A PAC invests resources in building capacity of members. The return on investment takes a substantial period to be realised.

Activities (Practices and Procedures)

Stapenhurst et al. (2005) and Ngozwana (2009) suggested that certain practices and procedures play an important role in enhancing a PAC's effectiveness and improving its consistency and effectiveness. McGee (2002, p. 72), for example, states that '[c]ommittees that meet on a frequent basis have a better opportunity of promoting consensual working practices than committees whose members cone together infrequently'.

Because PACs do not examine policy issues, they generally confine themselves to hearing evidence from departmental officials rather than ministers (McGee, 2002). It can reasonably be assumed that representatives of government agencies, statutory authorities and representatives of government-owned corporations are senior public servants that have sufficient understanding of the issues PACs examine.

The empirical evidence regarding the importance of some PAC outputs, noted by Hedger and Bliss (2008) – number of committee meetings, number of committee hearings and number of reports issued – is far from conclusive, however. Nevertheless, as we have shown, these outputs are related to each other, suggesting that a PAC which is productive in one area will be effective in others.

Ngozwana (2009) argues that planning enables PAC members to think, visualise, clearly understand, and document what they need to achieve, and how and when they will achieve it and, in so doing, to help accomplish a PAC's objectives and goals. Planning should also form an integral part of a PAC's day-to-day activities including prioritising its workload, planning and conducting meetings and hearings, reporting, following up on its recommendations, and assessing achievement of its performance measurement. Attributes proposed by Stapenhurst et al. (2005) were:

- **The committee meets frequently and regularly.**
- **The typical witness is a senior public servant (the 'accounting officer') accompanied by the officials that have detailed understanding of the issues under examination.**

Planning and conducting meetings

Committee meetings are important forums through which, among others, audit reports are considered, hearings planned, and professional development matters discussed. McGee (2002, p. 75) notes that some PACs around the Commonwealth use subcommittees to give a support service to the main PAC, especially to prepare a work programme that the PAC can adopt. The attribute proposed by Stapenhurst et al. (2005) was:

- **A steering committee plans the committee's work in advance and prepares an agenda for each meeting to the full committee.**

Ngozwana (2009) drilled down and suggested several working practices to accomplish this attribute:

Planning for a meeting

- The purpose of planning for a PAC meeting is to ensure that the meeting can achieve the intended results/outcomes. The Chair should assume a leading role in planning a committee meeting and must be supported by the Clerk and committee members. The planning process covers the following activities:
    o Defining the purpose of the meeting and setting goals, objectives, and intended results.
    o Sending meeting notices and agenda to all members of the committee well in advance.
    o Timely distribution of relevant background documents and minutes of the previous meeting to all committee members to enable them to prepare properly for the meeting. Advance preparation by all members will result in a productive and cost-effective meeting.

During the meeting

- The Chair, as the convener and facilitator of the meeting, must set a positive and productive tone among all committee members. Roles of the Chair include the following:
    o Explaining the goals and objectives of the meeting and ensuring that they are understood by all attending members.

- o Presenting and confirming the agenda.
- o Keeping participants focused and productive.
- o Encouraging objective participation by all members.
- o Maintaining a non-partisan environment and ensuring non-partisan decision making.
- o Providing a summary of the proceedings.

At the end of the meeting

The Chair –

- Summarises the major points discussed and resolutions made.
- Confirms actions and time commitments made.
- Announces the date, time and purpose of the next meeting.

After the meeting

- Minutes and transcripts of the meeting and an action plan should be distributed by the Clerk to all members (even those who did not attend the meeting) within 24 hours.
- All members should respect and observe deadlines.
- Each member with an action/s item should also try and develop a personal plan for accomplishing the action/s.
- The Chair or his/her delegate should follow up after the meeting to monitor progress.

Consensus

It is highly desirable to have a bipartisan climate within the committee. In some countries, there is an invariable rule that recommendations must be concurred in by all members of the PAC; this is the case in India, for example. In Australia and the United Kingdom, there are very strong conventions of PACs striving for unanimity in their conclusions, with very few instances of divisions or conclusions being recorded (McGee, 2002). Such consensus strengthens committee recommendations – and increases the probability of government acceptance. Thus we propose that:

- **The committee strives for some consensus in its reports.**

Meetings open to the public and media

Public hearings are a vehicle through which a PAC calls witnesses before the committee to provide testimony on critical issues raised in the audit report. It is also an important mechanism for public accountability, for verifying audit reports, and for increasing their objectivity and legitimacy of reports (Ngozwana, 2005). However, opinion is divided on whether PAC hearings should be open to the media and public. On the one hand, being open encourages parliamentary transparency, and it has been argued that the media not only provide valuable information for a PAC inquiry but also that its presence may also keep public servants and auditors on their toes and encourage more-realistic government follow-up. On the other hand, it has been suggested that open hearings may encourage political grandstanding by committee members and discourage bipartisanship (Messick, 2002).

Comments from the Study Group would support, on balance, that the advantages of public hearings outweigh the disadvantages. Stapenhurst et al. (2005) proposed, and we concur, that:

- **Hearings are open to the public; a full verbatim transcript and summary minutes are quickly available for public distribution.**

Ngozwana (2009) made some additional suggestions for planning an effective public hearing:

- Sufficient time should be allocated to hearings.
- Suitable briefing material should be made available to committee members prior to hearings to enable them to prepare and acquaint themselves with the main issues.

Measuring performance

As we show in this book, if the issue of measuring PAC capacity poses problems, the question of performance seems to be even more of an issue. Expanding on some initial observations made by Stapenhurst et al. (2005), Hedger and Bliss developed a possible framework for analysing PAC effectiveness (see Box 9.1).

When the number of activities (meetings, hearings, reports, inquiries) is correlated with the score that countries receive in terms of right of access, power, and operations, audit reports, we find that there is no relationship whatsoever between these powers and the amount of activity performed. When asked whether PACs have mechanisms to measure performance, most PAC indicated that they did not.

Study Group members highlighted many of the conventional performance measures such as an analysis of uptake by the executive from the recommendations of the Auditor-General and the PAC. Study Group members found the notion that actions have been taken on the basis of PAC recommendations was very satisfying. There were also comments about process measures such as the numbers and regularity of meetings. In addition there was the recognition that an effective PAC could contribute to reduction in waste and cost savings. However, this contribution is not always easy to measure.

At a structural level, the PAC could contribute to the quality of the public financial management in the country. First, it was recognised that the relationship between the PAC and the Auditor-General was critical and the performance of an effective PAC was reflected (at least in part) in an effective Auditor-General. Therefore, a PAC could support the independence, resourcing, and activism of the Auditor-General. This could also extend to recognition among accounting officers that they were eventually going to account to account to someone.

Regardless of difficulty, this suggests a new attribute, that:

- **A committee should assess its performance annually.**

Ngozwana (2009) suggested that the following performance indicators could be used:

- Number of Auditor-General's reports considered.
- The time lapsed between the tabling of the Auditor-General's report and the hearing.
- Number of committee reports produced.
- Number of hearings held per year.
- Recommendations approved or accepted by government.
- Recommendations implemented by government.
- Disciplinary action taken against officials who contravene financial administration policies and laws, as pointed out by the PAC.
- Compliance with laws and regulations subsequent to the PAC highlighting the shortcoming.

Resources

The issue of capacity is not only related to the mandate and scope of work of a PAC but also the staffing and financial resources available to PACs. Collecting information on the funding of PACs proved difficult. This was because, for many jurisdictions, no information was provided on funding. Moreover, those that did provide information are difficult to compare because of the differences in spending power between different countries. However, the financial resources (other than staff) provided fell into two general categories. Most jurisdictions provide some form of member allowance and travel costs. It is recommended that:

- **Committees should be involved in determining their own budgets. Such budgets should provide financial resources for member allowances, site visits and costs related to public hearings.**

There is a noticeable difference in the number of staff available to a PAC. There is a general relationship between the number of staff

Table 9.1: A possible framework for analysing PAC effectiveness

Inputs	Processes (and their immediate effects)	Outputs	(Intermediate) Outcomes	(Long-term) Impacts
Constitutional/legal framework	Conventions of conduct	PAC findings and conclusions (majority or consensus)	Sanctions and penalties applied to officials	Conventions and principles of conduct established for PAC
SAI role and inputs	Conventions of organisation	PAC reports and recommended actions	Improved financial systems and financial control	Culture of effective public financial accountability
Domestic stakeholder inputs (media, public)	Formalised working practices/modus operandi	Follow-up of recommendations (government response and implementation)	Increased financial efficiency of government	Culture of democratic accountability
Resources (staff, budget, infrastructure)	Intra-governmental co-operation between PAC, AG and Executive	Status reports on government actions	Improved public service delivery and public sector performance	Systematic feedback of outputs, outcomes and impacts into enhanced inputs and strengthened processes
International Co-operation				
Previous year PAC outputs (i.e., follow-up)		Public engagement and media coverage		
Conventions and principles of conduct			Effective legislative checks/constraints on executive power	

Source: Hedger and Blick (2008).

and the number of members involved in a PAC; small PACs have just a few staff, and large PACs have more staff. From a practical perspective, it seems to be important that a PAC has at least one dedicated staff member and that PACs who do not have dedicated staff support may struggle to perform their roles. This supports Stapenhurst et al. (2005):

- **The committee is adequately supported, with an experienced Clerk and a competent researcher(s).**

Study Group members argued that proper training and support for MPs who became PAC members. This might include local orientation training for new PAC members, mentoring from experienced MPs, plus courses on public accounts and performance auditing work on the practice of holding public hearings and how these can be best conducted. This suggests an additional attribute:

- **Specialised training (including orientation and mentoring) should be provided to new PAC members.**

BIBLIOGRAPHY

Hardman, D. J. (1984a) 'Canberra to Port Moresby: Government Accounting and Budgeting for the Early Stages of Devolution', *Accounting and Finance*, vol. 24, no. 2, pp. 75–97.

Hardman, D. J. (1984b) 'Public Financial Administration of Microstates: South Pacific Forum', *Public Administration and Development*, vol. 4, no. 1, pp. 141–54.

Hardman, D. J. (1986) 'Paradigms of Public Financial Administration in the Evolution of Papua New Guinea', *Public Administration and Development*, vol. 6, no. 2, pp. 151–61.

Hedger, E. and A. Blick. 2008. *Enhancing Accountability for the Use in the Public Sector Resources: How to Improve the Effectiveness of Public Accounts Committees*. A Paper Produced for the Commonwealth Auditors-General Conference held in Bermuda, July 2008.

Jacobs, K., Jones, K. and Smith, D. 2007. 'Public Accounts Committees in Australasia: The State of Play', *Australasian Parliamentary Review*, vol. 22, no. 1, pp. 28–43.

KPMG. 2006. *The Parliamentary Public Accounts Committee: An Australian and New Zealand Perspective*, KPMG, Canberra.

McGee, D. 2002. *The Overseers: Public Accounts Committees and Public Spending*, Commonwealth Parliamentary Association and Pluto Press, London.

Messick, R. 2002. 'Strengthening Legislatures: Implications from Developing Countries', PREM Note no. 63, World Bank, Washington DC.

Pelizzo, R. (2011) 'The Activity of Public Accounts Committees in the Commonwealth: Causes and Consequences', *Commonwealth and Comparative Politics*, vol. 49, no. 4, pp. 528–46.

Ngozwana, N. 2009. *Good Practice Guide for Public Accounts Committees in SADC*, Southern African Development Community Organisation of Public Accounts Committees (SADCOPAC).

Rawlings, G. 2005. *Regulating Responsively for Oversight Agencies in the Pacific*, Targeted Research Paper for AusAid.

Stapenhurst, F., Sahgal, V., Woodley, W. and Pelizzo, R. 2005. *Scrutinizing Public Expenditures*, Policy Research Paper 3613, World Bank, Washington DC.

Wehner, J. 2003. 'Principles and Patterns of Financial Scrutiny: Public Accounts Committees in the Commonwealth', *Commonwealth and Comparative Politics*, vol. 43, no. 3, pp. 21–36.

Afterword

In reflecting on both the origins and the activity of Public Accounts Committees (PACs), it becomes clear that there are two somewhat different objectives. On one hand, the PAC is a tool of oversight and good governance that will reduce corruption, and, on the other hand, it is seen as a tool of parliamentary accountability in the face of increasing managerialism and hollowing of the state. In addition, the nature and evolution of the PAC was institutionally specific and assumed certain political and social structures that might no longer be present or never established to begin with. In summary, the suggestion that an improvement in capacity will lead to an improvement in performance is dependent on these key assumptions.

Summarising the literature examined reveals a number of key themes and assumptions about the nature of PACs and the notion of what constitutes performance. First and foremost, the activity of the PAC is one element in a broader process of parliamentary oversight and audit. In order for a PAC to be effective, the other elements of parliamentary oversight and audit need to exist and be functioning, and the basis for this process is a shared understanding of the risks in the public sector. This interlinking relationship is clear from McGee (2002) but also from more-recent work by Wehner (2003) and Pelizzo et al. (2006). Therefore, the question of the capacity and performance of a PAC needs to be addressed at a systems level that considers the nature and performance of all of the elements of parliamentary oversight, most particularly the capacity and performance of the respective Auditor-General.

However, issues of risk need greater consideration, particularly in the interaction between a PAC and an Auditor-General.

The second key issue provides evidence for the primary role played by contemporary PACs. It is clear from McGee (2002), Wehner (2003), and Stapenhurst et al. (2005) that political neutrality and cross-party representation is a fundamental requirement for an effective PAC. This would suggest that the primary function of the PAC is parliamentary oversight and accountability. Both Pelizzo et al. (2006) and KPMG (2006) also provide evidence for this focus. They suggest that the primary measure of self-assessment and performance review is the ability of the PAC to impact government policy as measured by the number of recommendations accepted and implemented by the government. Certainly, the notion of measuring performance in terms of government acceptance and implementation of recommendations is consistent with the best practice for measuring the performance of parliamentary committees recommended by Monk (2010). However, this would suggest that the PAC's role of reducing corruption and misappropriation is receiving less attention. The danger is that what is measured is what comes to matter and what is not measured gets ignored, and the Study Group suggested that many factors need to be considered. This notion of a multifaceted approach to the understanding of capacity and performance is consistent with developments both in performance measurement (see Modell et al., 2007) and in democratic theory. Uhr (1998, 2001) argued that parliamentary committees provide an important forum for political deliberation. Therefore, issues of capacity and performance of PACs are centrally linked to their ability to function as a forum for political deliberation rather than to more-specific output in terms of the reports generated or the recommendations implemented. Interestingly, an informal discussion with individuals who has considerable experience as PAC staffers/committee secretaries in Australia also suggested aspects that underpinned the deliberative capacity of the committees. These included strong research and administrative support from a standing secretariat, a strong commitment from committee members and from the Chair to support open debate around issues of sound public administration, and the capacity of the committee to set its own work programme, to call witnesses and documents. This process required that the PAC provides a 'back-of-house' space for open deliberation while also presenting a 'front-of-house' presentation of bipartisanship and cross-party agreement. Clearly, such agreement and any notion of unanimity could not be reached without the respective 'domain of deliberation'. Again, we would suggest that considering issues of risk in a jurisdiction could provide a powerful framework for this kind of approach.

From a practical perspective, we suggest three things need to be considered. First, if the primary objective is the reduction of corruption and misappropriation, existing 'best practice' might not be the best practice at all. In fact, it may be necessary to develop some new and innovative approaches that strengthen this area. Second, it is necessary to take a systemic approach toward the issue of capacity and performance, which considers the place of the PAC in broader processes of parliamentary oversight. This needs to be a warning to those who consider implementing a PAC in isolation from these broader processes. In particular, a strong relationship with an independent and well-resourced Audit Office, including the capacity for regular private briefings, is a critical institutional link, as is the input from a PAC into a performance audit programme. And third, the power to examine accountings and financial affairs and to follow up both the financial and performance audit reports produced by the Auditor-General should be available to a PAC. PACs that lack these capacities would be encouraged to expand their mandate and powers.[35] While the examination of the efficiency, economy, and effectiveness of government policy can result in considerable political conflict, the capacity and practice of examining the efficiency and effectiveness of policy implementation is an important role for PACs. Again,

---

35. This would suggest, contrary to recent trends, that the issue of consideration of budget estimates would ideally be delegated to other committees where this is practical.

PACs who lack the mandate or capacity for this kind of work would be encouraged to take steps to address this obstacle.

From a performance-measurement perspective, care needs to be taken with the selection of formal and explicit performance measurements. While the question of the impact and take-up of PAC recommendations is important, it is also important to remember the role of the PAC as a critical domain of cross-party deliberation on issues of sound public administration. Perhaps future efforts to build capacity in this area could focus more on how the capacity for these processes of deliberative democracy are built and sustained.

BIBLIOGRAPHY

KPMG. 2006. *The Parliamentary Public Accounts Committee: an Australian and New Zealand Perspective*, KPMG, Canberra.

McGee, D. 2002. *The Overseers: Public Accounts Committees and Public Spending*, Commonwealth Parliamentary Association and Pluto Press, London.

Monk, D. 2010. 'A Framework for Evaluating the Performance of Committees in Westminster Parliaments', *Journal of Legislative Studies*, vol. 16, no. 1, pp. 1–13.

Modell, S., Jacobs, K. and Wiesel, F. 2007. 'A Process (Re)turn? Path Dependencies, Institutions and Performance Management in Swedish Central Government', *Management Accounting Research*, vol. 18, no. 4, pp. 453–75.

Pelizzo, R., Stapenhurst, F., Saghal, V. and Woodley, W. 2006. 'What Makes Public Accounts Committees Work?' *Politics and Policy*, vol. 34, no. 4, pp. 774–93.

Stapenhurst, F., Sahgal, V., Woodley, W. and Pelizzo, R. 2005. *Scrutinizing Public Expenditures*, Policy Research Paper no. 3613, World Bank Institute, Washington DC.

Wehner, J. 2003. 'Principles and Patterns of Financial Scrutiny: Public Accounts Committees in the Commonwealth', *Commonwealth and Comparative Politics*, vol. 43, no. 3, pp. 21–36.

Uhr, J. 1998. *Deliberative Democracy in Australia. The Changing Place of Parliament*, Cambridge University Press, Cambridge.

Uhr, J. 2001. 'Parliament and Public Deliberation: Evaluating the Performance of Parliament', *UNSW Law Journal*, vol. 24, no. 3, pp. 708–23.

Appendix: A Conceptual Framework

While the analyses of Chapters 3–6 provide rich empirical finds, they do not provide a conceptual framework for us to put the changing work of Public Accounts Committees (PACs). In this appendix, we present a conceptual framework for the study of PACs – heretofore, missing in the growing body of literature on PACs.

Legislatures have developed oversight tools to help hold the executive to account. The adoption of these tools by legislatures is influenced by 'path-dependent'[36] pressures and by the identification and adoption of good practice by one legislature from other legislatures (e.g. the adoption of Public Accounts Committees historically associated with countries with

36. Archetypical templates explain the initial adoption of legislative types. The notion of path-dependency is also useful – it suggests that certain institutional structures and processes will be mediated by the contextual features of a given situation, often inherited from the past, and will not follow the same trajectory nor generate the same results everywhere. Path-dependency assumes that there will be long periods of institutional continuity, which may be interrupted only at 'critical junctures' of radical change. At the same time, there is increasing evidence to suggest that there is convergence of legislative processes and structures through imitation. (The logic behind this is the belief that certain institutional processes or structures are beneficial and therefore worthy of imitation.) In sum, one would expect path-dependency to explain why some contextual factors (e.g., form of government and type of electoral system) are similar across countries, reflecting the initial template for design. But over time, there is movement away from the template, and the notions of convergence and mimetic isomorphism can explain similarities in legislative oversight institutions, despite different organisational templates.

'Westminster-style' parliamentary systems by legislatures in non-Commonwealth countries which have no political-historical ties with the United Kingdom). There is evidence to suggest that such adoption of good practice encourages legislatures operating in countries with different forms of government to converge, as they learn about each other's procedures and practices through bodies such as the Inter-Parliamentary Union and the Commonwealth Parliamentary Association.

But legislative oversight tools only partially explain legislative oversight, improved accountability and lower corruption. Stapenhurst (2011) found four contextual factors to be particularly relevant in shaping this context: the electoral system, public trust, political parties and type of government. A country's electoral system and form of government are often path-dependent. In developed countries they tend to be relatively fixed, having evolved over time (e.g. the United Kingdom) or have changed at a critical juncture, such as a change of constitution (e.g., France). In developing countries, electoral system and form of government are often adopted from the former colonial country (e.g., Ghana) or, again, have changed at a critical juncture (e.g., Nigeria). The evolution of political parties tends to be specific to a country's socio-political history. Public trust is also specific to a country's socio-political history and can perhaps best be explained by the concept of *social capital* (Madison, 1788; de Tocqueville, 2003; Bourdieu, 1986; Coleman, 1986, 1988). Fukuyama (2002, p. 27) defines social capital as 'shared norms or values that promote social co-operation'. Putnam (2000) argues that social capital is a key to building and maintaining democracy. From this perspective, one example of social capital is trust in the legislature, which, when sustained, installs and reflects 'social values' and enhances accountability. In this book, the notion of social capital is at least partly captured by the concept of political will. Institutional learning and adaptation also takes place by looking at how good practice elsewhere also influences context as institutions – such as Nigeria's National Assembly – copy the institutional structures and processes of other countries (in this instance, from the US Congress).

It is the *combination* of these theories that best explains legislative oversight, just as the empirical analysis indicates that it is the *combination* of oversight tools (including PACs) and contextual factors that explain legislative oversight (see Figure A.1). At the heart of the diagram are the PACs and other oversight tools and contextual factors. There is a two-way relationship between these variables. Contextual factors – such as form of government and level of democracy – influence the number of oversight tools available to a legislature (Pelizzo and Stapenhurst, 2012). There is some reason to believe that the greater number of oversight tools used by legislatures in parliamentary systems may reflect the relative weakness of contextual factors in such systems compared to presidential systems (Stapenhurst, 2011). Legislative oversight comprises both oversight tools and contextual factors and together these influence the efficacy of oversight.

This conceptual framework also lends theoretical support to Olson and Norton (1996, p. 6) who argue that external factors 'will largely determine [the capacity of the legislature] to exercise an independent influence in … policy making and that variables internal to it – along with the nature of the policy brought before it – will, at most, reinforce, but not determine that capacity'.

The framework suggests further that contextual factors are driven more by a country's social-political history than by notions of international templates associated with international best practice. Here, the concept of templates associates with archetypes and path dependency is important. For example, former British colonies now usually have a parliamentary form of government – a majoritarian electoral system – while former French colonies have a hybrid (semi-presidential) form of government and a proportional representation electoral system.

The framework also acknowledges the importance of social capital – public trust in Parliament, which acts as the glue which helps hold the framework together and political will.

APPENDIX

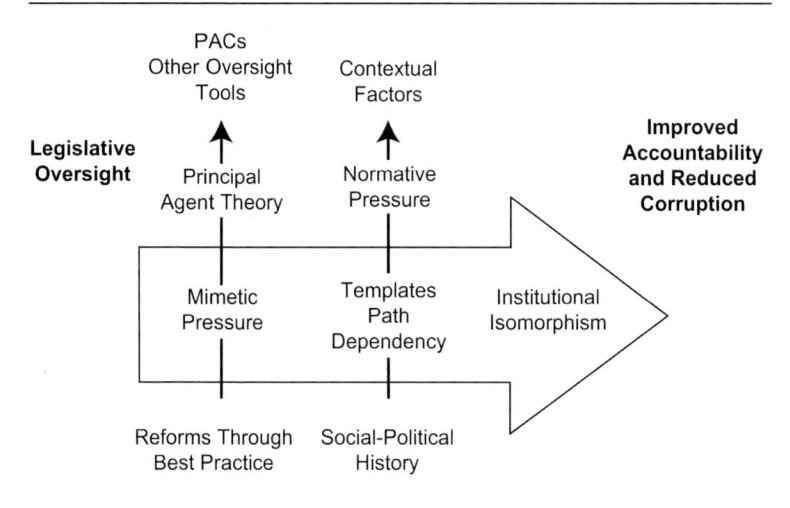

Figure A.1: Conceptual synthesis of legislative oversight

BIBLIOGRAPHY

Bourdieu, P. 1986. 'Forms of Capital', in Richardson, J. (ed.), *Handbook of Theory and Research for the Sociology of Education*, pp. 241–58. Greenwood, Santa Barbara, CA.

Coleman, J. 1986. 'Social Theory, Social Research and a Theory of Action', *American Journal of Sociology*, vol. 91, no. 6, pp. 1309–35.

Coleman, J. 1988. 'Social Capital in the Creation of Human Capital', *American Journal of Sociology*, vol. 94, pp. 95–120.

De Tocqueville, A. 2003. *Democracy in America*, translated by I. Kramnick. Penguin, London.

Fukuyama, F. 2002. 'Social Capital and Development: The Coming Agenda', *SAIS Review*, vol. XXIX, no. 1, pp. 23–37.

Madison, J. 1788. *The Federalist Papers* 37–58.

Putnam, R. 2000. *Bowling Alone: The Collapse and Revival of American Community*, Simon & Schuster, New York.

Stapenhurst, F. 2011. 'Legislative Oversight and Corruption: Presidentialism and Parliamentarianism Revisited'. PhD thesis, Australian National University, Canberra.

Index

This index is arranged alphabetically word by word. Tables, figures, and footnotes are distinguished by a lowercase t, f, and n, respectively.

accountability 19–20
activities
   measuring 138–139, 140t
   and PAC performance 53–59, 55t, 57f, 58f
   variation between PACs 48–53, 52t, 53t
   working practices 29–31
   see also best practice
ad hoc PACs 104–107
annual budget process 7f
Auditor-General 6, 8, 10, 11–12, 20–25, 66–67
   best practice 129–130
   independence of 21

balance of power 36
Baring, Sir Francis 9
benchmarks 14–16
best practice
   mandate and legal powers 123–129
   practices and procedures 133–139
   relationship with AG 129–130
   resources 139–141
   structure and organisation 130–133
   see also success factors

capacity and resources 74–78
   required for success 139–141
Chair (PAC) 10–11, 21, 27, 36, 38, 44
Commonwealth Parliamentary Association 19, 111, 149

executive *see* government

government
   relationship with PACs 6, 7f, 8, 8f, 12–13

hearings *see* activities
history 3–4, 8–10, 9n, 20

Index of State Weakness 85f, 86

legislative auditor 6, 8
   see also Auditor-General
legislature
   functions 5–6

relationship with auditor 8
tools 5–6

mandate
　of the AG 23–24
　of the PAC (*see also* powers;
　　right of access)
　　benchmarks 14
　　best practice 123–128
　　as a fiduciary obligation 8f
McGee, David 1–2, 18
meetings *see* activities
membership 26–28, 35–36
　size of 26, 35, 37–38, 40–41, 42t,
　　74–77, 76f

non-Commonwealth PACs 97–100,
　97t, 100–104, 100t

operation obstacles 13, 31–32, 43,
　44f, 45–46, 83–86, 84f, 85f
　overcoming 87–90
opposition (politics) 10–11, 15,
　26–27, 36, 37–38, 41–43

parliamentary oversight 110–113,
　143, 149–151, 151t
performance 34–36, 78–80
　judged by PAC activity 53–59,
　　55t, 57f
　measuring 138–139, 140t
　see also activities
policy 24–26, 65–66
political composition 10–11, 36,
　41–43

political will *see* parliamentary
　oversight
powers 12, 71–74, 72t, 73t
　transformation of 100–102, 101t,
　　102t
public financial accountability
　6–7, 7f

resources *see* capacity and
　resources
right of access 67–71, 68t, 70t

social capital 149–151
staff *see* membership
Stapenhurst, Rick 2
strategic interaction model
　113–117, 115f
studies on PACs 3, 4, 41t
Study Group 19, 20–24, 36–37
success factors 2–3, 37, 62–64
　see also best practice

terms of reference 11, 24–25
traditional-model PACs 94–96
　compared with non-
　　Commonwealth PACs 97t,
　　98–100, 100t
　departure from 100–104, 101t,
　　102t
　see also non-Commonwealth
　　PACs

Westminster model *see* traditional-
　model PACs
World Bank 36–37, 56, 106–107